THE POLITICS OF
PROJECTS

YOURDON COMPUTING SERIES
Ed Yourdon, *Advisor*

THE POLITICS OF PROJECTS

ROBERT BLOCK

FOREWORD by EDWARD YOURDON

YOURDON PRESS
A Prentice-Hall Company
Englewood Cliffs, New Jersey 07632

Library of Congress Catalog Number 83-070455

Printed in the United States of America

10 9 8 7 6 5 4 3

ISBN 0-13-685553-9 025

Prentice-Hall International (UK) Limited, *London*
Prentice-Hall of Australia Pty. Limited, *Sydney*
Prentice-Hall Canada Inc., *Toronto*
Prentice-Hall Hispanoamericana, S.A., *Mexico*
Prentice-Hall of India Private Limited, *New Delhi*
Prentice-Hall of Japan, Inc., *Tokyo*
Prentice-Hall of Southeast Asia Pte. Ltd., *Singapore*
Editora Prentice-Hall do Brasil, Ltda., *Rio de Janeiro*

to Susan and David

Honour and shame
from no condition rise;

Act well your part:
there all the honour lies.

Alexander Pope,
An Essay on Man, IV

Contents

Preface

For most of my adult life, I have been fascinated by political interaction. As an onlooker, I nod my head in appreciation of a deft maneuver much as a sports fan appreciates a skillful play by any player.

Upon entering the field of management, I realized that political interaction was not an optional activity, but rather a requirement of managers in any organization. As I painfully learned the skills of politics, it occurred to me that beneath the parries and thrusts of political fencing there was an underlying process, one that could be presented and taught to beginning and soon-to-be politicians. After more years than I thought it would take, the process is presented in this book. Since my career has centered on software development projects, the process is described in the context of these projects. But the concepts of political interaction extend to any political environment, and the process, with appropriate adjustments, should also apply.

This book includes a fictitious case study that I created and gleefully followed as its events transpired somewhat out of my control, and a step-by-step process that I hope you will follow until your own political process emerges. The book also provides some exercises, which follow many of the chapters. The exercises require paper and pencil and take five to ten minutes each. I suggest that you actually *do* the exercises, rather than simply read through them, since much of the learning you can derive from the book will come from reflection on your own political experiences while doing them.

Finally, I want to acknowledge my indebtedness to several people: to Tim Lister and Ed Yourdon for allowing me much of the time to write this book and for providing the personal computer on which to write it; to Rob Thomsett and Brian Dickinson for their input on project management; to Sue Barkhurst for her therapist's view of people and their motivations and for lots of patience; to Claudia Taylor for her cover design concept; to Lou Mazzucchelli, again to Tim Lister, and especially to III for their review of my manuscript; to Janice Wormington and Susan Moran of Yourdon Press for their editorial input, and to

Wendy Eakin for making readable English out of my sentences, and also for her encouragement, enthusiasm, and support.

And now I hope you enjoy reading the book as much as I enjoyed writing it.

Foster City, California   R.B.
November 1982

Foreword

At the tender age of twenty-two, I took a job as a programmer/analyst on a project that promised to revolutionize the way computers were used in hospitals. This was in the mid-sixties, when revolution was in the air, when we were all convinced that everything we did would have a profound impact on mankind. As it turned out, the project had a profound impact on me, but not on hospitals: After two years of intense effort, it was abruptly canceled.

The hardware and the software on that project seems primitive, almost Stone Age, by today's standards — but it was state of the art at the time. The staff was bright, energetic, and dedicated; among the entire staff of some fifty application programmers and systems programmers, I recall very few resignations or firings during the two-year period. And the project managers were fine, too; they made their mistakes, of course, but they were experienced and competent, and they knew what they were doing.

So why did the project fail? Simple: because of politics. *Politics*. The word is enough to strike terror into the hearts of computer programmers, systems analysts, and the bottom two or three levels of managers in any organization. Yes, we had politics, accompanied by all the human drama that one usually sees on television soap operas. Some marriages fell apart; some new liaisons began. A few overworked, fatigued technicians eventually suffered nervous collapse; others dropped out and joined a commune.

If only I had been older and wiser, I would have realized that it was great material — the stuff from which *The Soul of a New Machine* could be written.* But I wasn't very old, and I certainly wasn't very wise; in fact, I didn't have the faintest idea of what was going on . . . at

---

*T. Kidder, *The Soul of a New Machine* (Boston: Atlantic Monthly/Little, Brown, 1981).

least not in the political arena. Neither did my boss. Neither did my boss's boss, nor my boss's boss's boss. In fact, when the project collapsed, it became evident that not even my boss's boss's boss's boss — the manager of the entire multimillion dollar project — understood what, in retrospect, was a straightforward set of political maneuvers within a large corporation.

Ah, if only we had had available Bob Block's *The Politics of Projects* at the beginning of that ill-fated project. Reading it would not have helped me to affect the outcome of the project: I was a peon, low down in the hierarchy, with no political clout at all. But it would have given me enough perspective on the project to realize early on that it was doomed. Had I known that, I might not have worked twelve hours a day, seven days a week for two straight years. And maybe somewhere up the chain of command, a proper reading and appreciation of Block's stimulating book would have altered some critical decisions and turned disaster into triumph.

My disaster story took place in the mid-sixties, and Block's book is being published in 1983. It's tempting to think that *all* projects of yesteryear were disasters; it may also be tempting to think that *The Politics of Projects* is based on some revolutionary new theories that were just formulated last year. Neither is true: The project failure in which I participated back then is almost identical to the project failures I have seen several times a year since, in consulting assignments and travels through EDP shops around the world. Block's book is not based on any revolutionary new theory; it simply represents the culmination of many years of experience as a project manager.

The Politics of Projects will be a rude awakening for almost all newcomers to the data processing field, especially fresh new graduates, with their degree in computer science and a head full of programming techniques, theories of recursions, and other esoteric stuff. The reason for this is that Block starts right off with a categorization of the causes of failures in EDP projects; poor technical methods is only one of the causes — and a rather minor one at that. The major component in project failure, of course, is politics.

If the appraisal of project failures isn't sobering enough to the reader, Block follows it up with an even more dismal political reality: *Corporations don't need projects, they need systems.* As he eloquently points out, projects are a short-lived, artificial anomaly within the organization; they are tolerated only as long as the customer — the person or group who ultimately pays for the whole thing — has faith that all of the strange people, and all of the strange jargon, and all of the computer equipment, and all of the money will eventually lead to something he wants. If he loses faith, the project dies. Period.

None of the project managers I have met in the data processing industry has received any formal training in the politics of projects; whatever these managers have learned has been through osmosis, and through bitter, painful experience. More important, the vast numbers of fledgling programmers and analysts (from whose ranks most project managers eventually emerge) usually have no idea that politics is an inevitable phenomenon whenever two or more humans interact; consequently, their mood during the course of a typical project ranges from bewilderment to sullen resentment at the realization that "management doesn't know what it's doing."

In my opinion, *The Politics of Projects* should be required reading for all participants at every level of a data processing project. The book is clearly stated, easy to read, and full of commonsense suggestions. It has a case study that you will swear was taken from your organization; in a sense, it *was,* because all EDP projects share basically the same political problems. Most important: You should read Bob Block's book because it offers convincing evidence that one doesn't have to succumb to "the dark side of the Force" (as Obi-Wan Kenobi put it) in order to be aware of, and to be an astute player in, the political process. When you finish reading, you'll understand just why this is so, and you'll be a better player in the game of politics.

New York City   Ed Yourdon
February 1983

THE POLITICS OF
PROJECTS

1

WHY SYSTEMS FAIL

If I define a successful system as one that is developed *on time and within budget;* is *reliable* (bug-free and available when needed), and *maintainable* (easy and inexpensive to modify); *meets its goals and specified requirements;* and *satisfies the users,* how many of you would say that your organization builds successful systems? I've asked this question of hundreds of people at all levels of data processing, and the overwhelming response is one of silence. Occasionally, a hand will rise or someone will say "well, sometimes," and once in a great while all members of a group will say "we do." But the vast majority of us have worked on systems that do not meet these criteria for success — in other words, on systems that in some way can be classified as failures.

I raise this issue of success because political problems are often the cause of failure in building systems. This is recognized intuitively by most of us, but the extent of the political impact is rarely appreciated. As a beginning for our discussion of the politics of projects, we will explore this connection between politics and the failure to build successful systems. We will do this by first looking more closely at the reasons for failure and then examining the contribution of politics to failure.

1.1 Reasons for failure

Based on my observations over the years and the experiences of the students in my seminars, I have identified a set of twelve categories into which we can classify most system failures. The categories of system failure are resources, requirements, goals, techniques, user contact, organizational, technology, size, people management, methodology, planning and control, and personalities. As you read through the discussion of the categories below, try to find examples from your personal experience that fit each category.

1.1.1 Categories of system failure

The first category to examine is that of *resource failures*. Resource failures involve conflicts of people, time, and scope; that is, the people and the amount of time allotted are not sufficient to build the required system. These failures are most often due to imposed deadlines combined with an inability or unwillingness by management to provide adequate resources. Resource failures result in systems that are late and frequently over budget. Due to the time pressure, requirements are often compromised through haste and the use of improper techniques ("just get it done"), leading to incorrect systems with poor reliability, maintenance difficulties, and very unhappy users.

Incorrect, incomplete, or unclear specification of system requirements leads to *requirement failures*. Poor specification of requirements results in development of the wrong system (that is, a system that does the wrong things or doesn't do the right things) and therefore leads to dissatisfied users. When the problems are discovered, many changes may need to be made to the system; if the changes are requested prior to system implementation, schedule and budget problems may result.

Goal failures result from inadequate or incorrect statements of the system goals by management, or from a misunderstanding of the goals by the system builders. Since the misstatement of goals puts system builders on the wrong track, they may try to build a system that is not needed. This leads directly to incorrect specification of requirements and all of its consequences.

Technique failures are failures by the system builders to use, or to use correctly, effective software development disciplines such as structured analysis and structured design. If poor techniques are used throughout the system building process, the result is inadequate specification of requirements, poor reliability, costly maintenance, schedule and budget problems due to implementation difficulties, and dissatisfied users.

User contact failures are caused by an inability to communicate with the user community. The user may be someone within the organization, a customer outside the organization, or all potential customers constituting the marketplace. When the user is within the organization, user contact failure is often a cause of faulty specification of requirements and leads to poor preparation for acceptance and use of the system by members of the user community (they don't want it and don't know how to use it properly).

When the user is an outside customer, communication is weakened by the explicit organizational separation of developer and user and by pressures to get the job done ("take the money and run"). Poor requirements become fixed by contracts, and time pressures lead to compromised techniques. The customer often receives a poor product that barely meets contractual acceptance criteria and is difficult to change.

When the user is the entire marketplace, a surrogate user, possibly from the marketing department, guesses the needs of potential customers. System requirements are usually ill defined and frequently changed. If the surrogate user is wrong, the system will be poorly received by the marketplace.

Organizational failures result from an inability of the organizational structure to support the system building process. The failures can be internal or external to the system building group. Within a system building group, either lack of leadership or an excessively large span of control will cause confusion and floundering, with group members pulling in various directions, possibly negating each other's progress. If the group is large and requires multiple subgroups, failures can also result from poor coordination of tasks between the subgroups. In either case, the system building effort can experience schedule delays and result in products of inconsistent quality.

External organizational failures result from the system building group's poor relationship with the DP development organization around it. Unclear or multileveled management reporting relationships can lead to little or no effective management control, review, or direction. Functional, rather than project, partitioning of the development organization can cause fragmentation of control and excessive subcontracting of portions of development efforts to people with other responsibilities and priorities. In the extreme, lack of clearly designated responsibility for a system development effort can lead to disinterest by any subcontractor or to battles for control of the system's development. This confusion and squabbling often results in serious schedule delays and budget overruns.

Technology failures are failures of acquired hardware or software utilized by the system. The hardware or software doesn't work as described in its specification, the vendor is unable to meet the delivery schedule, or the product is unreliable. Usually, these failures involve new hardware or software products that have not been thoroughly tested. Vendor support may also be a problem for new software and new hardware; and for software packages, future enhancements may be very difficult. In the worst case, technology failures can result in schedule delays, poor reliability, maintenance problems, and disenchanted users.

Although *size failures* can almost always be attributed to several of the other categories, the root of the problem is that the system is too big. Big systems are usually functionally complex, and tend to push the system development capabilities of an organization to or beyond its limits. In this latter sense, bigness is relative to the capabilities of the organization. An organization that typically builds systems requiring less than ten person-years to develop will need entirely new methods to deal with a one-hundred person-year system.

Size failures in many ways are manifested by insufficient resources, incomplete requirements, simplistic project control, inadequate techniques and methodology, and a lack of organizational structure, leading to the problems described in each of these categories.

Failures to motivate workers and to maintain the morale of the system building group are *people management failures.* The resulting lack of effort, stifled creativity, and antagonistic attitudes have an impact similar to that of internal organizational failures, only in this case, the fault lies not with the organization but with the group leader. People management problems lead to time delays and budget overruns (an inefficient, nonproductive staff rarely delivers on time or within budget), poor specification of requirements, and an unreliable and unmaintainable system.

Methodology failures are failures to perform the activities needed to build the system: Unnecessary activities may be performed, needed activities may be omitted, or activities may be performed incorrectly. Methodology failures may be due to the lack of a formal methodology as a guideline to the system builders, or to an overly rigid adherence to the adopted methodology. The consequences can affect any of the success criteria, depending on the specifics of the failure.

Planning and control failures encompass planning, scheduling, task assignment, and tracking of results. Included here are vaguely defined assignments, inadequate tools to depict plans and schedules, and failure to track progress to insure that tasks are done.

When a project is poorly planned and controlled, the members of the system building group are not sure what they are supposed to do or when they need to be finished. Work assignments often overlap, deliverables are ill defined, and everyone feels vaguely uneasy. In large system efforts with multiple subgroups, communication of schedule changes and task completion may suffer, leading to poor coordination between subgroups and the passing of misinformation to upper management. Planning and control failures lead most frequently to schedule delays and budget overruns.

Personality failures are clashes between people either within one system building group or between group members (often the leader) and members of an interfacing organization; the failure results from people disliking each other enough to prevent them from doing their jobs. In the extreme, acts of sabotage and vengeance may occur, but more often there is passive cooperation and covert resistance.

The impact of these failures varies with the functions and assignments of the individuals involved. They are rarely catastrophic, but often aggravate already difficult situations.

1.2 Internal and external problems

Some of the failures can be dealt with from within the system building group by its designated leader. Others seem to be less controllable. For example, the leader can pay more attention to the proper use of a given technique, monitor task completions more carefully, or spend more time with the group members to improve morale, without any need to get management approval or deal with people outside the group. Other problems, such as management's unwillingness to provide additional time or resources, its rigid insistence on use of a methodology package, uninvolved users, or incomplete requirements provided by a formal customer, appear to victimize the system building group and seem beyond the control of the group and its leader. I call problems within the control of the group leader *internal* problems, and problems requiring approval, action, or decision by persons outside the group *external* problems.

While internal problems are not easy to solve, external problems involve an additional dimension − dealing with people who are not subject to the decisions of the system building group leader. Solving external problems requires getting people to change without being able to issue orders. This step enormously increases the difficulty of the problems.

1.2.1 The external component

To better understand the contribution of external problems to system failure and success, I've assigned each of the failure categories an *external component,* a number on a scale of 0 to 10 that indicates how each category of failure is influenced by external factors. The higher the number, the greater the external influence, with the 0 rating indicating no external component, and the 10, no internal component. In other words, the external component is an indication of how often system failures are a result of external problems, problems whose solution requires interaction with and decisions by people outside the system building group. As you read the following, pencil in your own external component rating number where it differs from mine.

> *Resources:* Unless the resource allocation was based on estimates made by the system building group, resource problems are entirely due to external management decisions. Primary here are preset deadlines, fixed resources, and unwillingness to reduce scope of the system development effort. **9**

> *Requirements:* In many cases, the system building group does a poor job of defining requirements even though all needed input is available. More often, specifications are incorrectly provided by an outside group or inadequate or wrong information was provided by the users. **6**

> *Goals:* Unless the system building group misunderstands or ignores the goals provided to it, goal failures are external; goals are either vaguely defined, wrong, or nonexistent. **8**

> *Techniques:* The use of proper software development techniques ought to be an internal decision, but is an external one when management prevents use of proper techniques by insistence on old standards, or by refusal to properly train people or to support the use of the techniques. **4**

> *User contact:* When users are available to the team and their knowledge is not utilized, this is an internal problem. Most user contact problems, however, involve unwilling, uninterested, or unavailable users. **9**

> *Organizational:* Organizational problems within the system building group are relatively infrequent unless the group is large enough to require multiple subgroups. Inefficient upper management control and fragmentation of system development responsibilities are much more common. **9**

Technology: Selection of hardware or software products almost always involves people outside the system building group, and it is selection of the wrong products that leads to the failure. **9**

Size: Usually, the pressures for a big system come from the user and from DP management. However, there are some cases in which the group leader has authority to control or establish system size and allows the system to become too large. **8**

People management: The organization's way of doing things, its culture, can influence and pressure the system group leader into bad people management practices. But a skilled leader can usually provide good people management in spite of outside forces. **2**

Methodology: This is a hard one to call. The lack of a methodology or, more commonly, rigid standards forcing use of a methodology that doesn't fit the system development needs, is an external problem. But the leader often has some discretion, an ability to customize the methodology, that he or she does not exercise. As with people management, there may be lots of pressure to do it wrong, but the leader still has the option to do it right. **5**

Planning and control: The enforced use of a clumsy control tool might cost some overhead, but this area is still under the leader's control. **1**

Personalities: When clashes are within the group, I call them internal; when they involve people who are not group members, I call them external. Most are external. **7**

Table 1.1 depicts the failure categories and my external component ratings. I've tried to order the categories by frequency of occurrence, but most systems experience multiple causes of failure, so any ordering is very rough.

Table 1.1
System Failure Categories

Category	External Component
1. Resources	9
2. Requirements	6
3. Goals	8
4. Techniques	4
5. User contact	9
6. Organizational	9
7. Technology	9
8. Size	8
9. People management	2
10. Methodology	5
11. Planning and control	1
12. Personalities	7

What emerges may be somewhat shocking. If the categorizing and rating is anywhere near valid, we are forced to conclude that *the external component of failure is the major contributor.* Each category of failure except for people management and planning and control is greatly influenced by external factors. This indicates that the system building group leader must apply a great deal of attention, time, energy, and skill to dealing with external factors. It also implies that a leader who practices good people management, uses good control techniques, and has reasonable ideas about software techniques may still lead a system building effort that fails miserably for a wide variety of reasons.

1.3 The political component

In my view, the external component is the *political* component. When a project is beset by political problems, forces external to the system building group are pushing the development effort toward one or several of the situations identified within the failure categories. Coping with the political forces is often critical to the success of the system and the group responsible for its development.

People given responsibility for leading system building groups are, in general, ill equipped to deal with these external political components. They probably have spent much of their careers developing technical skills, and while elevation to a leadership role implies some predisposition to interact reasonably well with peers and management, preparation for this portion of the job by means of formal training, informal discussion groups, or even reading material is virtually unknown. The leaders are thrown into the deep water and required to sink or swim on their own, along with the systems they are to build.

If the leader of a system building group is to cope with problems driven by external forces, he must be able to interact politically. In this book, I discuss the political component, and then introduce an approach toward more successful political interaction in the project environment.

To help illustrate the situation, Chapter 2 begins the saga of a company and a system building group struggling with its assignment to develop a system.

Chapter 1: Exercises

1. On a grid layout similar to Table 1.2 below, list all the systems you have worked on or have watched from a good vantage point.

2. Rate each of the systems against the success criteria on a graded scale of 1 to 5 (where 1 is poor and 5 is excellent).

3. Assuming that at least some of the systems were not totally successful (not all 5's and 4's), consider each unsuccessful system. Identify the failure categories that apply and whether they were internal or external. Pay particular attention to your current or most recent system. If the failures and problems are internal, train yourself and your project team in the structured techniques, people management, project control, and structured methodologies. If the problems and failures are external, finish reading this book.

Table 1.2
System Success Evaluation

System	On Time/ Within Budget	Reliable	Maintainable	Meets Goals/ Requirements	Satisfied User
ABC	4	2	1	3	1
XYZ	1	2	1	1	2
FMP	3	4	3	4	4
ALPHA	...	...	...	...	...
YMISIII	...	...	...	...	...
GLOTZ	...	...	...	...	...
......	...	...	...	...	...
......	...	...	...	...	...
......	...	...	...	...	...
......	...	...	...	...	...
......	...	...	...	...	...
......	...	...	...	...	...

2

A CORPORATE
EXAMPLE

2.1 Smoot Industries: Act I

Although I believe that we learn best by personal experience, we also learn by example. To this end, I have given brief life to a set of characters engaged in the struggle to build a system. I have tried to create a typical organization: one of average size, with a broad range of people encountering typical problems and situations. Hopefully, their actions illustrate some common problems and will help you to see how the external (political) component contributes to the potential failure of system building efforts. The company and the people are entirely fictitious, but the actions of people in comparable situations are remarkably similar, so you may be reminded of companies and people you have known.

2.1.1 Setting the scene

Smoot Industries is a middle-sized manufacturer and distributor of motor vehicle parts and supplies. Its customers are the major automotive firms; bus, truck, and off-road vehicle manufacturers; and, recently, Uncle Sam. Smoot was formed in 1946 by three ex-Service mechanics who saw an opportunity to build a successful company during the post-war economic boom. In Smoot's more than thirty-five years of existence, it has grown to respectable size, with manufacturing centers in Detroit, Los Angeles, and Newark. It is recognized as an aggressive and successful competitor in its field.

Smoot is headquartered in New York City, where the corporate data center is located. The data center is responsible for all software development and maintenance and for central-site computer operations. In addition, there is a small operational data center at each of the manufacturing sites. By corporate edict, all three manufacturing centers use the same systems whenever common processes, such as production control or inventory management, exist.

Of particular concern to our story is the Inventory Management System. The current system is fourteen years old. It is the third-generation extension of the original set of manual procedures and tab equipment processes set up in the mid-fifties to handle the Detroit manufacturing center, prior to Smoot's expansion to the East and West coasts. Processing is now fully automated, tab equipment having been eliminated fourteen years ago.

While the inventory system was never one to write home about, modifications and enhancements over the years have made it an absolute nightmare to maintain and operate. In addition, increased competition, the current recession, and the growth of Smoot have made it essential that its $200 million inventory of raw materials and parts assemblies be managed more efficiently.

To this end, management hired the consulting firm of Lawrence, Morris & Curlan to study the system and recommend an alternative. True to form, LM&C completed its four-month study by delivering a two-part report — an executive summary and a detailed design — prepared on the finest stationery and handsomely bound, with both LM&C and Smoot logos embossed on the cover. Following a presentation to the Systems Management Committee (SMC), twenty copies of the report were handed over, and LM&C passed GO, collected its $200 thousand, and went home.

The report recommended that the existing system be completely replaced, with the core of the new system being a material control package marketed by an LM&C affiliate. The new system would operate at the three plant sites on a set of minis connected to the mainframe system in New York, and would feature the latest in online, integrated database, and distributed technology.

LM&C estimated that $800 thousand would be needed for software development plus the package, and estimated that the system would take fourteen months to implement and install. The new system was to be called System Control for Reporting, Inventory Management, and Planning, or SCRIMP (a name that particularly pleased Curly Curlan, the corporate acronym ace). LM&C projected that SCRIMP would reduce Smoot's inventory by tens of millions of dollars.

The Systems Management Committee was delighted. Following the presentation, the committee members congratulated T.J. Woods, vice-president of Information Systems, for his selection of LM&C and the fine job it had done.

Woods was given fifteen copies of the report for immediate action. He in turn passed the copies down to John Hardmyer, director of Systems and Programming, letting him know that the SCRIMP project should be initiated immediately with whatever resources were available.

2.1.2 Action

Enter our hero, Bernie Stone. Bernie had been a senior programmer/analyst at Smoot for almost three years, and was finally getting his big opportunity: a promotion to manager and control of the hottest project in the shop. If he succeeded with SCRIMP, Bernie knew that his career would be on its way. Ralph Johnson, manager of Systems and Programming, passed copy number 11 of the LM&C report to Bernie and indicated that he could store it in his new office on the following Monday.

Johnson told Bernie that the LM&C report was very complete, and that upper management felt it would solve the company's inventory problems. The pressure from above was tremendous and SCRIMP had top priority. Johnson went on to say that project team members, all of whom would work for Bernie, had already been chosen, and they would be told of their new assignment following the announcement of Bernie's promotion on Friday.

Bernie Stone was impressed. This was the first time he could remember a development group being formed so quickly. He would have seven people initially, with three more programmer/analysts added following the installation of the new Accounts Payable System in two months. His team included Frank and Alan, two programmers hired a month earlier who had, respectively, one and two years of DP experience; Jack, a senior programmer/analyst recently demoted from manager due to the instability of his systems (he had maintained the existing accounting systems); Judy, a former program librarian upgraded to programmer trainee and given five weeks of intensive training; and Jerry, Marsha, and Sam, the maintainers of the existing Inventory Management System.

Johnson had assured Bernie that even though Jerry, Marsha, and Sam were to continue maintaining the existing system, he would hold changes to an absolute minimum to keep SCRIMP on target. He added that because Bernie's team was a bit smaller than LM&C had recommended, the date for the new system's installation would be moved from fourteen to sixteen months. "And as further help," Johnson continued, "even though user requirements have been thoroughly defined by the LM&C study, Charlie Parsons from Purchasing will be assigned half-time to the group for the first five months. He will help resolve any questions about inventory terminology or operations."

"And don't forget," Johnson continued, "SCRIMP will be the first system developed using the new FORMS* methodology package. We know it will help and we're counting on you to bring SCRIMP in on time."

The feelings of excitement and satisfaction associated with a first major promotion are usually accompanied by fear about whether the new job will be too difficult. Bernie Stone experienced this concern as he was about to change his status from worker to boss, but his worry was not specifically related to SCRIMP and the probability of its success. The details of SCRIMP would wait; first, there was the satisfaction of being chosen, the enhanced status, and the excitement of the new job.

Absorbed in his newfound bliss, Bernie was not fully aware of the maneuverings that had taken place between the time of the SMC meeting and his new assignment. After a lengthy discussion, Hardmyer and Johnson had decided to use SCRIMP to get authorization for an additional manager (Bernie). Staffing for the project was, however, another matter. Even though SCRIMP had approval and priority, there were no funds budgeted for the hiring of new people. As a result, the SCRIMP team was limited to the unassigned programmers and analysts in the department (two recent hires, one demoted manager, and an upgraded librarian). Consequently, the current Inventory Management System maintenance group was thrown in, with outstanding maintenance requests moved to the back burner. This still left the project several people short of its recommended number, so three people would be transferred from the Accounts Payable project following its completion.

---

*Formal Operations and Required Methods

In spite of these problems, Hardmyer felt that the SMC would demand installation of SCRIMP close to the LM&C suggested deadline, and negotiated sixteen months as the available time, regardless of the resources given to the project.

Johnson reluctantly agreed. He recently had been entertaining the idea of early retirement, and so wasn't willing to do battle over resources. He rationalized that Smoot often had resource squeezes such as this one, but at least SCRIMP had the LM&C report to guide it. And, in any case, it would be Stone's problem, not his. . . .

3

SYSTEMS,
PROJECTS,
AND POLITICS

Before returning to Bernie Stone's struggles to build SCRIMP, we need to define some terms and concepts about the system development environment.

3.1 Defining systems, projects, and their managers

Our discussion of project politics centers on projects, their teams and managers, and the systems that they build. As these terms are used here, SCRIMP is both a project and a system, the SCRIMP team is a project team, and Bernie Stone is a project manager. Because there are so many variations in the use of these terms, we need to define them clearly, starting with "system."

system   a combination of software, hardware, software packages, and procedures that performs a specific set of functions

"System" is a word that is in vogue today, and has a wide variety of meanings (the other day, I picked up a magazine and found a product described as a "running system" — it was a jogging shoe). My use of the word is limited to its data processing sense. For me, systems have the further limit that first, they use software to perform a major part of their function, and second, that most of the hardware involved is essentially computer hardware. But if you want to expand the definition to include your system's environment, go ahead.

Some further characteristics of systems are these:

- [ ] *Systems have goals,* either written, spoken, or implied. The goals usually identify, at some gross level, the system functions, interfaces, and the constraints under which they will operate.

- [ ] *Systems have users,* either belonging to the same organization that builds the system, to a specific customer, to a set of hoped-for customers (the marketplace), or to combinations of the above.

- [ ] *Systems have a life cycle* — conception, development, operation, and termination — and are very different creatures during each of these phases.

- [ ] *Systems are never right until they are history,* so during operation there is usually a need to fix or enhance the system; in other words, further development is done during operation.

- [ ] *Systems have names,* usually acronyms or three-to-four-letter combinations.

Because this book concentrates on systems during their development phase, and because it is during development that systems need projects, let's look next at a definition of "project."

project   the organized effort to (partially) build or modify a system

In the definition, I have included the word "partially" in parentheses to account for those system building efforts that are divided into multiple projects, either by system function or by development activity ("you do the requirements specification, I'll do the design and programming") or both. I refer to a project as the entire effort unless there is some reason to distinguish between partial projects and total projects.

Projects have characteristics:

☐ *Projects have goals,* either written, spoken, or implied, usually to develop all or part of a system, or to perform some meaningful set of activities needed for development of a system.

☐ *Projects have constraints,* usually limitations on the resources, budget, and time available to achieve the project goals.

☐ *Projects exist for a discrete period of time;* they will terminate when their goals are achieved (or when they fail).

☐ *Projects have identifiable users:* the users, customers, or surrogate customers (representing the marketplace) of the system.

☐ *Projects have names,* usually the name of the system they are to build followed by the word "project."

Projects require people to staff them. In most organizations, primary responsibility for a project is assigned to a group of people who work on the project and are presumed to have control over its destiny. These people compose the project team, defined as follows:

project team   the group of people whose full-time assignment is the development of the project's system, and who are generally regarded as having responsibility for the entire system development effort

Often, specialized groups or individuals perform specific tasks or major activities needed for development of the system. While these people may be considered to be working on the project, they either are not full-time members, are full-time members only for the duration of the specific tasks, or have a primary focus that is separate from the building of the system (for example, database designers derive data requirements from the system, but focus on incorporating that data into the entire integrated database). These people are not true members of the project team.

In organizations in which development is fragmented (usually functionally), multiple project teams for the same project may exist in different groups (for example, a user requirements team and a design/programming team).

Normally, a person within the project team is acknowledged by the organization as the leader of the group. This leader has responsibility for achieving the goals of the project. I call this person the project manager.

project manager   the person responsible for achieving the goals of the project and of its system

Titles vary widely. Depending on the organization, the responsible person may be called manager, leader, coordinator, or administrator of a project, system, application, program, or group. Regardless of title, the project manager has these responsibilities: achieving project and system goals; selecting project team members and overseeing their work; planning, requesting, and administering the project budget; interacting with DP management, users, and other non-team members; and administering team members' salaries. In other words, the project manager is the person in charge, the individual responsible and accountable for the project and the system while it is in development.

In some organizations, the project managerial responsibility is divided between two or more people, although all the responsibilities listed above still exist. Budgets and salaries are often controlled at a level above that of project manager, progress reporting is sometimes buffered by higher management, and, in matrix management situations, salaries may be controlled by the individual worker's administrative manager. In large projects, the size of the effort may dictate a leveling of responsibilities by partitioning the system into subprojects and by separating the various project functions, resulting in a hierarchy of project managers.

When I refer to the project manager, I mean the person having this total set of responsibilities. In organizations in which the responsibilities are partitioned, the reference applies to the set of people who have the project manager's responsibilities. When I refer to a specific subset of the responsibilities, such as work direction, then the reference applies to the person who has this portion of the responsibilities.

With these basic definitions as a foundation, we can now proceed to a discussion of politics and political interaction.

3.2 Defining politics

To most people, politics is a dirty word. And the people who engage in politics are seen as Machiavellian manipulators, who scheme toward their own immoral ends. The politician is feared, held in awe, and disliked. His motives are suspect, and he can never be trusted. In fact, there seems to be a belief that, at the governmental level, the politician is always working at cross-purposes to the good, moral goals of decent people. In the business environment, behaving like a politician is slightly more acceptable; people in positions of power within an organization are expected to be manipulative and to work toward their own ambitions at the expense of the organization's goals.

But if bad guys play politics, what do good guys do? What do you do when things aren't going your way and other people control or influence their direction? Is it any different from what people do who happen not to agree with your position?

If we turn to the dictionary, we find politics defined as relating to governmental activities or, less frequently, to scheming for power within any group. Some dictionaries include as a rare meaning the totality of interactions between people. This last definition is better, but none of these definitions seem to characterize the interactions in a way that helps us to understand the process involved.

If we limit politics to mean only those actions that are manipulative and dastardly, taken only by people with whom we do not align ourselves, then we not only lack a word for what the rest of us do, but we also are unable to look realistically at what is involved in political interaction and how we might cope with the external (political) component of failures. In other words, we need a term to describe the interaction between people when they are trying to change each other's behavior or opinions.

Rather than search for a new word, I propose that for the reading of this book we suspend prior definitions of politics and adopt a definition that is more useful for looking at the process involved:

politics those actions and interactions with people outside your direct control that affect the achievement of your goals

The definition is personal and active. It applies to actions that you take to achieve your goals (including doing nothing).

I have excluded interactions with people under your direct supervisory control. These interactions are entirely different from political interactions in that you have the authority to tell these people what to do. Consequently, the process involved is different and should be dealt with separately.

Notice that nothing has been said about the morality of the action and interactions; the process itself is neither good nor bad, it is simply a process. It is the use of the process that can be judged.

When I speak of politics, then, I am referring to interactions between people trying to get their way, without implying that these actions are good or bad. Political interaction in this sense is unavoidable — we all do it. We do it when we attempt to sell anything, when we are involved in negotiation, when we try to convey our ideas to others, when we try to develop some future plans or policy with others. We do it at our jobs, in our homes, with our friends, in any organization in which we have a say. Political interaction in this sense is a common activity, and while it can be manipulative, in general *it is not.*

3.3 Project politics

This definition of politics extends beyond the project environment and beyond the business environment to all areas of interaction. Without modifying its nonjudgmental nature, we can limit its scope to include only projects:

project politics   the actions and interactions between project team members and people outside the team that have impact on the success of the project, its system, the project team, and the project manager

The definition excludes interaction within the team between people under direct control of the project manager. It extends the scope of interaction to include those interactions that affect not only project and system, but the team members and the manager as well. Most of us would not sacrifice ourselves for the good of the project, and so interactions with consequences to the individuals involved are included within our scope.

This definition says that whenever we are involved in interactions outside the team boundary that will affect, or that we think will affect, the success of the project, the system, or the team members, we are engaged in project politics. The focal point of this interaction is most often the project manager, but team members also get involved depending on how the manager chooses to delegate responsibility.

Some of the more typical political activities are these:

presentations — requests for approval and funding, formal and informal presentations of plans and schedules, progress reports, system overviews, including what the system will do or is doing

reviews — technical critiques of content, standards, impact, and conformance to regulations or procedures

interviews — investigations to determine how things work or should work

interface negotiations — decisions on the software or hardware interfaces between systems

subcontracting — requesting, monitoring, and receiving software, hardware, materials, specifications, and other required products from non-team members either within or outside the organization

product delivery — delivery of externally required plans, specifications, and other products, including any portion of the system

memos, phone calls, and miscellaneous contacts — communication with people involved in the above activities

Political interactions are taking place all the time, and they involve a rather considerable list of people and groups. Each project has its own cast of players, but a typical project includes

direct management — anyone from immediately above the project manager all the way up to the level at which project funding and approval are given

user management — anyone responsible for specification of goals or for system approval in any of the user organizations, including surrogate users and customers

working-level users — anyone whose job responsibilities and activities may be changed as a result of the system, or who has responsibility for specifying detailed processing policy. Again customers and surrogate users may be involved. In some cases, working-level users may also be user management in that they have responsibility for approving the system.

peer-system project teams — team members and managers who develop, modify, or maintain systems that interface with yours

vendors — sources of hardware, software, and materials needed by the system

internal subcontracting groups — groups with delegated responsibility for delivering intermediate products or portions of the system. Examples of products are database design, installed hardware, user training materials, and acceptance test sets.

test teams — teams responsible for integration testing, acceptance testing, or other forms of system testing

EDP auditors — internal and external groups with responsibility for insuring proper system controls

internal support groups — groups responsible for monitoring and controlling standards, techniques, methodology, required procedures, or system impact on hardware and software

external regulatory groups — organizations or governmental agencies that administer laws or regulations affecting the system

quality control groups — any group that verifies content and technical validity of the system

consultants — people who may serve in any of the above roles

If you refer back to the reasons for failure presented in Chapter 1 and their frighteningly large external component, you will see that minimizing the external component of failure means improving the kinds of interactions you have with the groups or individuals listed above. By including these interactions and groups, our definition of project politics provides the proper context for dealing with the external failure component. If we can examine and better understand the process of dealing with this component, the political process, we will be able to use it to reduce the causes of failures, and so move toward more successful systems.*

---

*Chapter 6 examines this process.

3.4 How the organization views a project

Organizations do not need projects, they need systems. Unfortunately, systems that utilize today's computer technology require that people with specialized skills and experience in the use of the technology be employed to build the systems. The people who need the systems (the users) in general do not have these skills and experience and find it impractical in terms of time, energy, and predisposition to acquire them. In short, to build systems, users need experts.

In most organizations, a specialized group is responsible for system development (and ongoing maintenance). This group is separate from computer operations and other production functions and from the end user. This development organization (which may cross departmental boundaries) consumes the bulk of the data processing expense budget, employs most of the programmers and analysts, and consists of a set of development and maintenance projects.

So this thing that nobody really wants — the development project — constitutes a large and powerful portion of the corporate organization. In addition, it spends a lot of money and has enormous impact on the success or failure of the organization as a whole, based on the quality of the systems that it builds.

But let's keep our perspective. The project is a necessary device to get what is needed: the system. Unfortunately, the project, unlike most tools, is complex and unpredictable. Its members think, make decisions, and are fallible; and, unfortunately, most development organizations have track records that are anywhere from so-so to awful.

So, in the eyes of the user, the project takes on an alien, necessary evil quality. It is needed but not trusted, and, at the slightest hint of problems, becomes even more suspect.

The project is a temporary device to achieve the installed and operating system. In defining and building the system, the project necessitates spending large amounts of money. It is responsible for making and remaking user policy (as expressed by the system's processing logic) and for physically changing the way in which the policy is carried out (as expressed by the system's interface between people and the computer). This is all done with techniques incomprehensible to most users by a group beyond their control.

This user-view of projects is a key element in the politics of projects. It is the user who keeps us in business, the user who stands to rise or fall based on our product, and, therefore, it is the user with whom we must cultivate the best working relationship.

3.5 What we have said

We now have some definitions and a common understanding of system, project, project team, project manager, and politics as the terms are used in this book. And, we should have a new perspective about projects. They are in business to serve the user, but are themselves unwanted. As long as project teams are doing the job properly and are perceived to be doing so, they will be allowed to continue. But when the job is being done poorly or is perceived as being done poorly, the project becomes vulnerable to change, and rightly so.

The underlying message here is, Pay attention! Understanding the people you are in business to serve is the first step toward success. Cultivate a relationship with your users, let them know you care, and be sure that you do care that their system will do the things that they need done, as simply and quickly as possible.

Chapter 3: Exercises

1. Develop a parallel set of definitions for system, project, project team, and project manager that fit your organization. What constitutes a system? a project? Can you identify project teams? How are the project manager's responsibilities distributed?

2. Consider some of the political moves (including those you consider manipulative) that you have observed involving any of your projects. Put yourself in the place of each person who made a move. What would you have done in each situation? What were the motives of each of these people? What would your motives have been?

3. Consider your current or most recent project, and look at the project through the eyes of each major user, taking on his background, skills, and pressures. What does the project look like? Is the interaction between you (the user) and the project satisfying your needs and giving you confidence in the project? If not, what could be done to improve that interaction? What options do you have if the project becomes suspect?

4

TAKING CONTROL
OF A PROJECT

Suppose that next Monday your boss calls you in and says that in one week you are to assume control of a major system development effort. In other words, you are being made project manager. What do you do?

Most likely, what to do is not described anywhere in your company. The job description of project manager, if indeed one exists, was probably written by someone from Personnel and bears no relationship to the job as it has been practiced, and your predecessors in this role are not likely to have recorded their experiences or advice.

4.1 How to begin

Taking on the job of project manager is serious business. Projects run from several months to years in duration and consequently have long-term career implications, whether they succeed or fail. As a beginning, there are two questions that need to be answered: Will you accept the job? and, Exactly what does the job entail?

Fortunately, you are in a good position to assess the situation. You have the fresh outlook of a beginner, with the ability to assess the reality of the situation as an unbiased outsider.

Even though nothing has been written specifically to prepare you for the job, people have led system building efforts in your organization before. These past efforts are precedents for the way your organization conducts projects, and they provide the source information for your evaluation.

The initial evaluation of a project and its system should consider five areas:

☐ the rules for system building
☐ the players
☐ the goals and constraints of the project and system
☐ your responsibility and authority
☐ the feasibility of success

Each category needs to be carefully assessed and understood in order to make the decision to accept the job, and in order to begin planning and doing the job.

4.2 The rules

Determining the rules for building a system is relatively straightforward. It is simply a clarification of the process of conducting projects. The process includes the methodology; required project control; procedures for review, approval, and funding; and protocol for user interaction. Each of these areas is defined briefly below:

methodology   the set of activities and products required of projects. If no formal methodology exists, the practices of other project managers generally establish the precedent for these activities and products.

project control the systems and procedures, if any, required to track task completions and expenses against schedule and budgets

review, approval, the procedures for obtaining funding, re-
and funding ceiving approval for progress to date and future plans, and formal reviews and presentations required by any groups or individuals

user interaction the procedures for contacting users, includ-
protocol ing interaction with coordinators, bosses, and others whose permission you will need

You need to understand these areas well enough to follow correct procedures and to spot any serious problems that would affect your conduct of the job.

4.3 The players

If people already have been assigned to the project team, you should evaluate them carefully, considering their qualifications, their performance on this or any other project, and their personalities. These people are your basic work force, and if they are not properly qualified or performing well, they will decrease your chances for success.

Also consider the players external to the project team. Analyze the groups that will be involved with the project. Groups to consider are all potential user organizations; your direct management, including those people or groups responsible for funding and approval; auditors and other review groups; subcontractor groups; and vendors.

The issue is to understand the support or resistance you are likely to receive from each of these groups. Two perspectives to consider are your relationships, positive or negative, with members of these groups, and the opinions or public positions taken by members of the groups relative to your project.

4.4 The goals and constraints of the project and system

The fundamental question here is, Can the goals of the project and system be met within their respective constraints? Answering the question requires an understanding of the goals and constraints of both project and system. A formal charter may exist defining these goals and constraints. If not, you need to quickly assess them. In either case, it is essential that you understand what you are being asked to do and the limitations with which you will have to live.

Using Table 4.1 as a guideline, identify the specific entries under each subheading for your project. This should give you a reasonable statement of the goals and constraints.

Table 4.1
Goals and Constraints

System Goals

- Functions
- Systems to replace
- Performance
- Reliability

System Constraints

- Hardware
- Software
- Packages
- Environment

Project Goals

- Required products
- Productivity

Project Constraints

- Delivery dates
- Expense limitations
- Resource availability
- Facilities
- Logistics

4.5 Responsibility and authority

You are responsible for what management expects you and your project team to accomplish. Your authority is the set of tools and powers that have been vested in you, presumably to meet your responsibilities.

There are two types of responsibility: explicit and implied. Explicit responsibilities are the products that you and your project team are expected to produce, such as specifications, training manuals, operating software; and the activities that must be carried out, such as audits and acceptance tests. Implied responsibilities are more obscure; they relate to management's view of who is in charge or, to be blunt, who gets blamed if things fail. If you are viewed as in charge of the entire system building effort, you may be blamed for poor user training or installation of unreliable hardware even though you were not explicitly responsible for the training or the hardware selection. In this case, you have implied responsibility for all products that affect the success of the system building effort beyond those for which you have explicit responsibility.

Based on your observations and experiences, make a list of all products that you are expected to produce and all activities that must be carried out. These are your explicit responsibilities.

Next, consider the view of your management and that of your managerial users. How will they see you as project manager? What do *they* think you are responsible for? These responsibilities will probably be big items (such as successful operation of the system as a whole) and their perceptions will be affected by how you interact with them (for example, if you are the one who reports periodically to management on project progress, you are likely to be identified as the person in charge — or at least the most likely scapegoat).

When you feel satisfied that you understand management's perspective, make a list of things that management may blame you for that are beyond your direct control, things that other people or groups normally do that will affect your activities and products. These are your implied responsibilities.

Your authority is the set of tools and powers vested in you. These tools and powers enable you to control the variables that govern the size of the system to be built, the project team doing the building, and the system building process in which it resides.

Up till this point, we have focused on the way things are (or how they will be, if you accept the job). Authority focuses on what you are allowed to change.

The factors we have discussed define the environment that you are about to enter as project manager: the methodology; the project control mechanisms; the procedures for review, approval, and funding and for user contact; the players, including your team, management, users, subcontractors, vendors, and auditors; the goals and constraints of system and project; and, finally, your responsibilities, explicit and implied.

All of these can be considered variables, and your authority is your ability to make changes in any or all of these areas. Review each area and ask yourself what, if anything, you are allowed to change.* Examples of questions to ask yourself follow:

- Can you customize the methodology to suit your project needs? Can you delete activities? Can you add activities?

- Do you have the authority to hire and fire team members? Can you train them?

---

*Keep in mind that to change does not necessarily imply to perfect, but rather to adjust or modify. So there may be some areas in which you don't have the authority to create the ideal, but you do have the authority to improve the situation.

- Do you have control of goals and scope? Can you say no to an excessive requirement?
- Can you select qualified user analysts for your team? Can you determine which users to interview?
- Do you have control over due dates and schedules? Can you adjust tight deadlines?
- Can you partition the system into pieces?
- Can you reject poor products produced by subcontractor groups?
- Can you evaluate packages before using them?
- Is the review, funding, and approval process rigid, or can it be modified to fit your project?

The appropriate questions to ask depend on your project's environment. Their answers constitute the detail of your authority. Be aware that some of the answers may be wrong: You are dealing in many cases with issues of culture and precedence, and your answers are based on your observations and those of your associates. Your impressions may be incorrect and the culture may be changing. So, your actual authority and what you think your authority to be may not be the same. If you overstep your boundaries, the difference will be apparent, but if you underestimate your authority, you may never realize what you could have done.

4.6 Feasibility of success

Now that you have defined the project environment and your authority to control it, refer back to the reasons for failure outlined in Chapter 1. Ask yourself which types of failure are likely to affect your project. Make a list of the problems you find. In some cases, the importance of individual problems changes when they are combined with other problems. For example, the inflexibility of a deadline may not be too serious until you discover that the project team is very inexperienced and that no money is available for expanding the team or training team members.

Assess the potential consequences of each problem or problem cluster. What is likely to happen if the problem is not resolved? In some cases, the consequences are relatively easy to identify. In others, the impact is much more subtle. For example, the consequences of a geographically spread set of users may lead to initial inputs from local users that do not represent those of remote groups, leading to subsequent rejection of the system or major changes to it when users in remote locations find the system unsuitable for their needs.

Now consider your authority. For each problem with its potential consequences, is your authority adequate to resolve the problem or improve the situation until it is acceptable? In other words, compare potential solutions to your perceived ability to effect them.

At the beginning of the chapter we posed two questions: The first was, "Will you accept the job?" and the second was, "Exactly what does the job entail?" The process described in the chapter really gives an initial answer to the second question, the answer being used for your decision on the first question. If you do decide to accept the job, this answer is also the source for what needs to be done when you begin.

Chapter 4: Exercises

1. Consider your present or most recent project as if you were about to take on the assignment. Evaluate the project as described in this chapter. Now consider the project from your current vantage point. How valid would your initial perceptions have been? If the project is succeeding (or has succeeded), how were the problems corrected? If not, what could have been done to correct the problems?

2. Chapter 2 introduced Smoot Industries and the SCRIMP project. Evaluate SCRIMP according to the steps discussed in this chapter. Identify SCRIMP's problems, potential consequences, and Bernie Stone's authority to solve them. Before reading Chapter 5, decide whether you would take the job as SCRIMP's project manager.

5

SMOOT:
ACT II

Before resuming the odyssey of SCRIMP, let's look a little closer at the Smoot organization. The three founders, Chuck McLear, Albert Straus, and Harold Kahn, met in the Service. They took an immediate liking to each other, realized they had a set of skills that meshed nicely, and set up shop in Detroit near their primary source of business, the major auto makers. McLear, a mechanical engineer, gravitated toward manufacturing; Kahn, an economics and marketing man, leaned toward business matters; and Straus, with his MBA, took over the role of president.

In 1960, Smoot expanded to the East Coast and, two years later, to the West Coast. As both Straus and Kahn were native New Yorkers, they moved Smoot's headquarters to Manhattan when the eastern manufacturing center was opened in Newark.

In 1975, Kahn retired, and his hand-picked successor, Bob Kappler, took his place as group vice-president, Administration and Finance. Kappler in turn filled his former position of senior vice-president, Finance, with Arthur Gold, Smoot's best money man. Soon after taking his position, Kappler yielded to the suggestions of Smoot's major client and moved R.A. Barnwell III from vice-president, Contract Administration, to senior vice-president, Administrative Services. Barnwell had engineered a successful new contract with the client, and Kappler promoted him and retired his predecessor.

Unfortunately, in addition to contracts, Barnwell's new role included responsibility for the Information Systems organization, an area about which his knowledge was seriously limited. Kahn had cautioned Kappler about this, but in retirement Kahn's opinions were not sought as eagerly as before.

Barnwell moved Jackson Taylor-Smith into his vacated Contract Administration slot; and when the vice-president of Information Systems resigned in 1976 because of personality conflicts with Barnwell, he hired T.J. Woods as the replacement. A year later, Woods split his organization in two, sliding its top man, Matt Fitzmorris, over to director of Computer Operations, and promoting John Hardmyer to director of Systems and Programming. The current Smoot organization is shown in Figs. 5.1 and 5.2.

Since 1977, Information Systems had been relatively stable, although rumors persist in Systems and Programming about Ralph Johnson's possible early retirement and about his likely replacement.

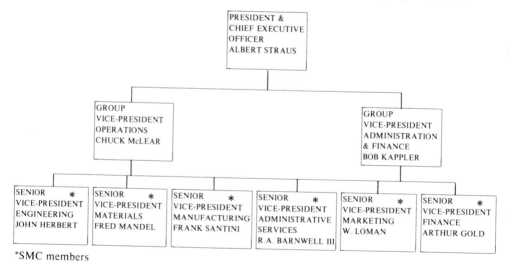

Figure 5.1. **Smoot corporate organization.**

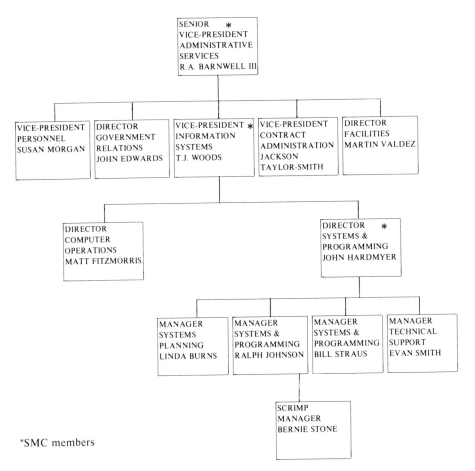

*SMC members

Figure 5.2. Smoot administrative services.

5.1 Meanwhile, back at SCRIMP

While Bernie Stone had heard the rumors about his new boss's possible retirement, he certainly had not entertained any ideas about getting the job. Bernie was up to his ears in SCRIMP.

It had been one week since the announcement of Bernie's promotion. On the first Monday, the team members assembled and began working together. Each received a copy of the LM&C report and read it from cover to cover. On Wednesday, they assembled again to discuss the system and their ideas and concerns. By the following Monday, Bernie was able to assess both the system and his team, and by the deep frown on his forehead, it was clear that the honeymoon was over.

The team itself was far from being the best group ever assembled. Frank looked promising, but Alan, the other new programmer, seemed weak; Jack would make a contribution as soon as he recovered from his demotion; Judy, the former librarian, had much to learn, and would be using this project as her primary training ground; Jerry, Marsha, and Sam had good knowledge of the existing system, but of the three, Marsha turned out to be the only sharp one; and Charlie Parsons turned out to be a total loser, with a very specialized knowledge of purchasing and a general lack of understanding about systems, and whose accumulated half-time amounted to one half day during the first week.

During the evaluation meetings, Marsha raised some questions about the LM&C requirements, expressing concern that they seemed quite different from the current system and indicating that the users might have to change the way they do business in order to use SCRIMP. She said enough to cause Bernie to invite his friend Steve Silva from Inventory Planning and Control to a review session. In the Materials organization, Inventory Planning and Control was the group responsible for controlling inventory levels and would be a key user of SCRIMP. Yet Silva had not even *seen* the LM&C report. It seems that LM&C had preferred to work on its own, and even now only one copy of the report had found its way into the entire Materials organization. As far as Silva knew, no one there had reviewed it.

With Silva's help, Marsha and Bernie began to uncover some very big problems. Their review lasted the rest of the week, but by the session's end, a clear picture emerged. Their observations follow:

Resources: The LM&C estimate required twenty person-years to do the job. To meet the schedule, SCRIMP would have to add eight people to the existing team (including the three late arrivals from the new accounting system).

Package: The software package at the heart of SCRIMP did not fit Smoot's environment. Major changes would be required either to the package or to Smoot's way of doing business. The package required new user terminology, and the SCRIMP database would have to be kept separate from other Smoot systems. In addition, the Smoot Part Number could not be used by SCRIMP, the package appeared to value the inventory differently, and it did not carry enough detail for proper cost management of the manufacturing processes. In all, seventeen changes, some of them quite extensive, would be needed to make SCRIMP compatible with Smoot.

Requirements: Except for the package, user requirements were vague, consisting of general statements about function and excessive detail about files and programs. A serious effort would be needed to define remaining user requirements.

Cost justification: While everyone believed that a new inventory system was needed, no one wanted to commit to benefits. SCRIMP had not one dollar of hard benefits to its name; the "tens of millions" in savings were pure fiction.

Compatibility: Future systems at the manufacturing centers would not be able to use SCRIMP terminals unless changes were made to their software, and even then potential capacity problems might exist.

The picture of SCRIMP that emerged was grim. Given the current constraints, if the developers were to implement SCRIMP with the changes and the further definition they believed necessary, the system would be a minimum of two years late and at least one million dollars over budget. And, they would have to live with an inventory database permanently separated from manufacturing and other systems, with the possibility of side-by-side terminals, one for inventory and one for other inputs. The situation was clearly unacceptable.

Stone, who normally slept like one, turned into an instant insomniac. As soon as he had identified and documented the SCRIMP problems, he sat down with his boss, Ralph Johnson, to discuss them.

It's hard to know what Bernie expected, but certainly not the indifferent double-talk he heard. Bernie described all the findings as clearly as possible. But, instead of providing a sympathetic ear, Johnson first insisted Bernie was wrong, then reverted to downplaying the differences, and finally said that LM&C knew what it was doing and if Bernie couldn't handle it, maybe someone else could.

As we already know, Johnson really did not care about SCRIMP. He had some concern for the spot Bernie was in, and perhaps saw some truth to his claims, but Ralph Johnson was soon to become free, and this was not going to be his fight. Anyway, Hardmyer and especially Woods (who had picked LM&C) would not hear of problems with SCRIMP.

If Bernie Stone had had insomnia early in the week, during the night following his meeting with Johnson he never closed his eyes. Fortunately, it was Friday, giving him the weekend to recover.

5.2 Rude awakening

Bernie had always operated under the assumption that people did reasonable things. And if decisions proved to be wrong, then a simple statement of facts would clarify the mistakes and begin the process of correcting the decisions. But, barely one week into Bernie's first job as manager, his boss slammed the door on reason.

He spent Saturday walking. Bernie took his job seriously, and could not shake his problems. First, there was the fear of failing, and a possible quick end to his managerial career. Then, there was anger — at Johnson for his unwillingness to see the very serious problems. And finally, after these emotions had dominated Bernie for most of the day, he reached a new understanding of the situation.

Bernie was a fast learner. Many people upon encountering a brick wall at high speed will continue to pound their head against it, complaining in their spare time about the headache. Bernie, on the other hand, did not like pain. One encounter was enough to cause him to look for doors, ladders, or paths around the wall.

That Saturday, he realized that not everyone's motives and actions agreed with his — that selfishness, greed, anger, stupidity, and other personal motives often got in the way. And while he did not like that realization, he knew that moaning while the ship sank would not keep anyone from getting wet. As a result, in one short afternoon, Bernie learned his first political rule: Observe and accept the reality of a situation as it is, and then make the best of it.

The second political rule, that tenacity and persistence usually win in the long run, was one that Bernie did not need to be taught; tenacity had been a part of his personality for as long as he could remember.

His new awakening complete at least for now, Bernie arrived at his office Monday ready for battle. And while he still didn't have answers, he now had clarity of vision.

On that Saturday, he had realized that Johnson didn't give a damn, probably because of his early retirement plans. He also realized that, because Woods had hired LM&C, he would not accept the possibility of problems with their study or report, and that Hardmyer, owing his promotion and current job to Woods and not being well liked by anyone else, would not be willing to see the problems either. The unpleasantness of installing a poor system would bother them less than facing the problems, since installation was sixteen months or more away and since neither had Bernie's insight into the seriousness of the problems.

At lunch, he discussed the situation with Steve and Marsha and, after some headshaking, Silva proposed another path. Although Silva did not work directly for Fred Mandel, senior vice-president of Materials, he knew him reasonably well and might be able to arrange a meeting with Bernie. Because the Materials organization was a relaxed group, Steve's boss would not be upset by his direct contact with Mandel. And, if any group had a stake in the success of SCRIMP, it was Materials.

Bernie considered the suggestion carefully, realizing the risk of bypassing his entire chain of command. He didn't see any other alternatives: Project managers did not go before the SMC, so he could not air the problems there; his own management was blocking any direct action; and continuation of the situation was not acceptable. Steve believed that Mandel was a straight-shooter and would not put Bernie in unnecessary jeopardy, so Bernie agreed.

At 3:30 the next afternoon, Bernie quietly slipped into Mandel's office where Mandel and Silva were already waiting. When the group emerged at 6:00 p.m., Mandel was in a somber mood. He realized that SCRIMP as it now existed would be disastrous for Materials. By not offering user participation in the inventory study group, Mandel had blown it, and admitted this to Silva and Bernie. He had let Woods bring in LM&C and had ignored the entire study, effectively delegating his responsibility for a new inventory system to Information Systems (IS). It was accepted practice at Smoot to let IS do the systems work, but systems were now such an enormous part of any operation that Mandel realized it had been a serious mistake. Once he understood the damage SCRIMP would do to his organization, he decided to take back his responsibility.

As a member of the SMC, Mandel called an emergency meeting with SCRIMP as the only agenda item. At the meeting, he announced that Materials had conducted an analysis of the SCRIMP report, and let Silva give a detailed presentation. When Silva was through, Mandel said that the LM&C report was so deficient he could not accept it. Rather, he proposed that another study of Smoot's requirements be conducted, this time by Smoot itself. In recognition of the IS role in system development, Mandel suggested that the IS SCRIMP manager (Bernie) lead the study, but that he report to Mandel, who would also fund it, for the duration of the effort. Materials would provide Steve Silva as a member of the group, and would request participation by Manufacturing, the other principal user of the inventory system. Mandel had approached Frank Santini, head of Manufacturing, prior to the meeting and Santini had immediately agreed.

Mandel had done his lobbying well. In the time between his session with Bernie and Silva and the SMC meeting, Mandel had personally contacted Santini, Gold, John Herbert (senior vice-president of Engineering), and Bill Loman (senior vice-president of Marketing), so that no one except Barnwell, Woods, and Hardmyer was surprised. His recommendation was quickly approved and the meeting adjourned.

With one quick stroke, Bernie Stone had pushed the right button. He had taken on a disastrous assignment and, with a good deal of luck, he had helped turn it into a rational one (the new study was Bernie's idea, although Mandel had inserted himself as overseer and funder). The world looked rosier, but Bernie had permanently and swiftly crossed the line between naiveté and political awareness — and it would never be quite as rosy as before.

As an aftermath to the meeting, T.J. Woods resigned. Barnwell immediately explored instituting court action against LM&C, but Jackson Taylor-Smith advised that the contract was binding even though Smoot did not like the product. With $200 thousand paid to LM&C, Barnwell identified the easiest scapegoat and accepted Woods's resignation. To fill Woods's slot, John Hardmyer was named acting vice-president of Information Systems — a slot he accepted in a cold sweat, pleased that he still had a job, although he wasn't sure what "acting" meant.

Ralph Johnson regained interest in his job, suddenly seeing the prospect of a promotion with Hardmyer's potential move up. A couple of weeks later, he put two and two together, and wondered if Bernie Stone had done anything to cause Mandel's move. But there was no way to find out, and it didn't really matter.

As the curtain closes on Act II, the SCRIMP Requirements Study team is in place, located in a conference room just outside Mandel's office. The team is headed by Bernie and includes Steve, Marsha, Ernie Smith (an Eastern Manufacturing Region industrial engineer), Jack Hoffman (also from the SCRIMP team), and Harold Newton (Mandel's budget analyst, who is to help identify the projected benefits of the new SCRIMP). The remaining members of Bernie's original team have returned to maintenance of the existing inventory system or have been assigned to other areas in IS.

5.3 What's going on here?

With the end of Act II, it is worthwhile to re-examine exactly what happened. How did things proceed from awful to good?

Bernie had found himself in a bad situation: He was a political neophyte, thrown into a disastrous situation, with no opportunity to evaluate the job before he accepted it and limited tools to deal with the problems once he started the job.

When Bernie accepted the job, he certainly was pleased at his new status and recognition, not to mention his raise. But he also took on the assignment with the idea that he would do a good job, and that he and his project team would build a system that would meet the success criteria described in Chapter 1. It's unlikely that Bernie verbalized this, but we can see that he believed that a well-done professional job is rewarded and is personally satisfying.

From the outset, he worked in concert with his users, instinctively realizing that he was in business to build their system, even though they (Mandel and the Materials organization) were not even looking. So when he, along with Marsha and Steve, discovered Pandora's box lurking inside the LM&C report, he went to his boss with the problem. This was mistake number one: He hadn't realized that Johnson didn't care, nor that IS management would not allow mistakes to be found.

Fortunately, the mistake was harmless, Bernie's plea merely being rejected (although he did not improve his standing with Johnson). And, here is when Bernie got smart. He changed his perspective, realizing that things are not always as they should be, and he began to evaluate the situation as it really was. With his limited knowledge, he did so very well.

He recognized the IS blockade and his inability to approach the SMC directly. At that point, he got lucky. Bernie had seen no other viable alternatives until Steve Silva suggested the meeting with Mandel. It worked, but was quite risky and could have backfired in many ways, depending entirely on Mandel's reaction.

Like many first-time managers, Bernie knew almost nothing about the people and responsibilities outside of his organization. He had never been to an SMC meeting, did not know Mandel, Santini, Gold, or any other members except by name, and the only people he knew in Materials were Charlie Parsons (for only half a day!) and his friend Steve Silva. And like many first-time managers, he had not considered other tactics, such as reducing the system scope, letting changes gradually ooze into the system, bargaining with his management for more of the IS resource, or pressuring LM&C to help make changes.

With additional knowledge or other tactics in mind, he still might have made the same move, which certainly worked. But it also resulted in Woods's firing, would delay SCRIMP for several months while the Requirements Study was conducted, and gave LM&C a (somewhat deserved) black eye. Most significantly, however, for the first time in Smoot history, the user organization became actively involved in and responsible for its own system requirements. On that basis, Bernie's actions deserve a medal. Bernie did not consider any of these issues, but the next time around (and there is always a next time around), he would be much more aware of possible consequences, good and bad.

And so, what we see now is Bernie Stone, his goals properly aligned with his users', discovering some serious obstacles to bringing in a successful system. After one quick lesson from his boss, Bernie realized the importance of properly perceiving the reality of his situation and of reading the other players. Finally, after evaluating a rather limited set of potential strategies, he got lucky.

Mandel, considerably more skillful politically than Bernie, has combined some good lobbying, one emergency meeting, and an intelligent proposal in order to dump the LM&C report. Unlike Bernie, he knows the other players well, immediately recognizing that Barnwell, Woods, et al., were unapproachable and in fact in an uncomfortable position, having paid for a rotten report. He also knows that Santini, Herbert, and McLear will support him in his move to get a workable system, and he is thankful that Stone and Silva approached him before he wound up on the wrong side in a losing battle.

5.4 Method to the madness

There is a pattern to the actions taken by Bernie and Mandel. Bernie's pattern is rather incomplete due to his inexperience, and Mandel's has become very intuitive, almost beyond his own cognition. If you asked Mandel how he maneuvers through the political mine field, he couldn't tell you — he just does it, and he knows that regardless of how well he does it there is an element of luck, because situations are rarely under any one person's control.

The process that Bernie is learning and that Mandel cannot explain is valuable and necessary in order to succeed as a manager in a project environment (or, in fact, in any other business environment). Sooner or later, in any project, events and sometimes people will conspire against the project and against the direction the manager wants to take it. And it is the manager's responsibility to keep the project on course, as he or she sees it.

The drop-out rate for first-time managers is high. As we noted at the end of Chapter 1, the reasons for failure have a frighteningly large external component, and new managers are generally ill prepared to deal with it. First-time managing is usually an ordeal by fire, and those who make it through generally have some scars to show for it.

The external or political component involves interaction with people outside the manager's direct control. Successfully dealing with this political component requires some variation on the process used by Bernie and Mandel.

Chapters 6 through 13 deal with this process. The process is dissected into its six component pieces, and each piece is discussed in detail. For the experienced manager, this should increase awareness of a process that is already being used. For the new or soon-to-be manager, it will help reduce the pain and time that learning otherwise takes.

6

THE POLITICAL PROCESS

Question: What portion of managers engages in politics?

Answer: All managers. By our definition of politics in Chapter 3, virtually every interaction that occurs between a person and the people who can influence the achievement of his goals has potential political impact. Refusing to play politics is itself a political move (generally, a rather poor one), so it's impossible not to engage in politics.

Question: What portion of managers is good at politics?

Answer: A very small portion. Generally, managers who have survived over the years, and particularly those who have risen toward the top, probably will be good politicians. Project managers who have delivered successful major systems have by necessity become politically skilled.

Question: How do managers learn to be good at politics?

Answer: Usually by trial and error, and most successful managers have the scars to show for it.

Question: Is it possible to learn the process less painfully, to become politically skilled without relying on the passage of time and on trial and error?

Answer: Not entirely, but by analyzing the elements of the process we can become more aware of political interaction and the possible ways to improve difficult situations. In other words, we can significantly reduce the learning period and the number of errors.

6.1 Inside the process

The political process for most people is a combination of conscious and intuitive, almost instinctive, actions. Those of us who are good at it either began with our intuition properly tuned or have learned over time where to look for trouble and what to do about it. The learned reactions gradually become assimilated and shift from conscious to intuitive processes. So, if you ask a politically skilled person how it's done, the answer will probably omit all sorts of actions that have become intuitive, and mention only those recently learned.

What's needed for the new manager is a partitioning of the political process into useful pieces that can be discussed and related to day-to-day events. These pieces should be relatively simple, and must be complete. The neophyte manager is not ready for sophisticated nuance, but needs to know the elements of the political process, to have a straightforward, step-by-step method for political interaction: a cookbook approach. As with any recipe, the approach given in this chapter should be used as is until its essential ingredients are understood; then it can be adapted to better fit the individual.

Over the past few years, I have observed the political process used by me and by people around me. Gradually over this period, I have extracted what appears to be a necessary and basic set of activities and have shaped these activities into a cookbook process. I field-tested the process myself, and compared it to the actions of other people. With this feedback, the process has been refined to the point at which I believe it can be used as a general guide for learning the political ropes. Keep in mind that this process, as with any general process, is a distillation of specific observations, and is only as good as the observations of the extractor. It works for me, but I suggest that you think about it, try it out in relatively low-risk situations, modify it to fit your style, and then use it to be more successful in your own political dealings.

Fortunately, most of the political issues in projects are relatively simple (having said that, I want to stress the word relatively, and also add that some issues can be very difficult). However, political interaction gets tough when both sides have something at stake, when a conflict will result in winners and losers. People will fight hard for their points of view against conflicting ideologies, when battling for promotions, or when attempting to protect publicly established positions. While these combative situations do arise in projects (Smoot's commitment to LM&C is an example), the typical project's political interaction is more mundane and easier to cope with. It simply amounts to doing things that other people need to have done in order to understand, approve, or cooperate with the project.

While the processes of combative and non-combative politics are basically the same, a rookie politician in a combative situation is likely to exit the loser, lucky if he survives to engage another day. The non-combative arena is a much better training ground because the political process can be learned there with lower risk.

6.2 Steps in the process

Isaac Asimov's wonderful science fiction epic *Foundation,* set millennia in the future, introduces a concept he calls psychohistory.* Psychohistory is the science of predicting what will happen on a galactic scale, based on the given circumstances of the universe and predictable reactions by the populace to stimuli and events. Asimov speculates that mathematicians and historians will work together and devise a scientific approach for predicting the future that successfully anticipates major changes in the course of events.

We are not, of course, in the business of predicting the future of the galaxy. Within the very small scale of a project, we are trying to do the same thing: to anticipate what is going to happen. While we will not use any mathematical predictors, our source of what's going to happen will be the players involved, their likely interactions, and resulting reactions and changes.

The purpose of the political process is to change situations and attitudes so that they are more in line with the project's goals. To do this, we first must understand clearly what our goals are and what they should be. We also must understand the environment, what is likely to transpire if things continue as they are, and what types of changes can be made to redirect the situation. From this assessment, we can formulate and then implement a plan to bring about the desired change. The process is imperfect, and so needs to be closely monitored and continually modified to deal with a changing reality.

---

*I. Asimov, *Foundation* (New York: Avon Books, 1951).

6.3 Overview of the process

I have partitioned the political process into six steps. Each step appears as a verb-object statement of what to do followed by a brief description. Don't be fooled by the apparent simplicity of the steps — each one requires discipline, insight, and energy. Some of the ideas discussed within the steps will probably be new to you. The steps first are presented here in brief, and then are described in detail in the following chapters. Although the descriptions apply to the project environment, the process itself can be generalized to apply to almost any environment in which political interaction occurs.

6.3.1 Identify goals

The political process should begin with goal clarification. There are two major types of goals to consider. The first type concerns the goals of the project and system. A project charter or some equivalent document that clearly states the goals of project and system helps, but the goals and intent of management must be understood regardless of what is written in any document.

The second major type of goal concerns the motivations of the project manager and, possibly, of the project team members. These may be looked at as personal goals; and if they are not aligned with the project goals (that is, if the manager or the team members are trying to build a system that is different from the one desired by management), there can be serious trouble. Many people do not have building a successful system as a primary goal, or even as a goal at all. Understanding personal goals is difficult, requiring introspection and observation of the team members.

6.3.2 Assess your capabilities

As project manager, you are at the center of most political interaction. To be politically effective, you need to understand your own style and the way you conduct yourself. This involves considerable introspection — regarding what you do, what you do well, and what you do poorly — in terms of the kinds of interactions that occur in political contact. The result of this step is an inventory of political skills you possess, as well as of areas that need work.

People tend to have ways of interacting that are effective and other ways that are irritating and, of course, ineffective. Usually, these ways of interacting are so automatic that we are not aware they exist; specific techniques are required to identify and evaluate them.

6.3.3 Assess the environment

This assessment is done in almost every political situation, usually intuitively and very often incorrectly. The process of assessing the environment has at least three subprocesses: understanding the formal organization, understanding the informal organization, and understanding the players. Understanding the formal organization is the most obvious and by far the easiest. Usually, an organizational chart and some research into the organization's system building culture can provide the information you need.

Understanding the informal organization is considerably more difficult, and involves discovering and identifying the relationships that exist between the players. In any organization, there are friendships, alliances, and other interrelationships that can potentially affect players' actions or points of view; these relationships are not identified on an organizational chart. The informal organization can have great impact on the decisions of any individual and must be understood if the outcome of any action is to be anticipated.

The third subprocess is the most important in assessing the environment: understanding each player's motivation in terms of priorities and values, with an eye toward an empathetic understanding. This kind of assessment is imperfect at best, and is made more difficult because people are always changing. The players must be continually reassessed.

6.3.4 Delineate the problems

Usually, any project in progress appears beset by a myriad of problems, to such a degree that the project manager may feel helpless and overwhelmed. This turmoil needs to be divided into relevant and irrelevant areas, and the relevant areas subdivided into discrete problems. This clarification itself reduces anxiety and allows more intelligent and concrete action to be taken. What results from this process is a set of problems germane to the project and its goals, many of which are at least partially resolvable.

6.3.5 Develop solutions

At this point, the information collected and presented in the preceding four subsections is used to construct a plan. A set of scenarios is devised to deal with the identified problems. Each scenario consists of actions and probable consequences of the actions. Probability of success and the consequences of failure for each scenario are evaluated, and the most appropriate course of action is selected.

6.3.6 Implement, test, and iterate

Any real-world process, including this one, is imperfect. This process includes recognizing the problems that exist for the project, understanding the players and their actions, and understanding your goals as they pertain to the project. The plan, or course of action, is based on these understandings and the changes that could occur when the plan is put into place. Any or all of these understandings can be incorrect, and the situation can change with time. When the plan is implemented, you must observe the impact of your actions and the interactions of the players, and continually evaluate the correctness of your perceptions and actions.

This evaluation may result in a reassessment of your goals and capabilities (steps 1 and 2, above). It may also require you to repeat your assessment of the environment, delineation of the problems, and formulation and implementation of new plans (in other words, an iteration through steps 3, 4, 5, and 6).

Political problems always exist, and continually change as a result of outside events and of the interactions between the players. So, this last iteration through steps 3 through 6, with occasional adjustments in steps 1 and 2, represents the normal situation. That is, the political process includes not only gathering feedback on the success or failure of a particular action, but also repeating the process itself.

6.4 Using the process

Figure 6.1 depicts the political process graphically. It identifies the six major steps and some of the substeps as well. The entire process is depicted as a loop to symbolize its iterative nature.

To some of you, the process may seem excessively rigid and procedural. You may feel that this is not how an experienced politician does it, and you are probably right. As noted earlier, most politically skilled people have assimilated the process. Lessons are learned slowly over time, and what was once a difficult lesson that required continual conscious attention soon becomes an intuitive response to situations. So, at no time did the politically experienced person consciously engage in our six-step process. At various times, however, elements of these steps were learned by repeated experience, until all or enough of the process became intuitive so that the person was politically competent.

The process is offered as a set of procedural steps. These steps will shorten the initial learning period, when so many costly mistakes can be made, and will provide a continuing reference. I suggest that you practice the process exactly as it is described here and in subsequent chapters, using the formality of the lists and activities as a discipline for doing it right. When you are comfortable with the process, your own style and approach will emerge and you will no longer need to adhere rigidly to these steps. But don't get careless; you will need to conform carefully to your own approach.

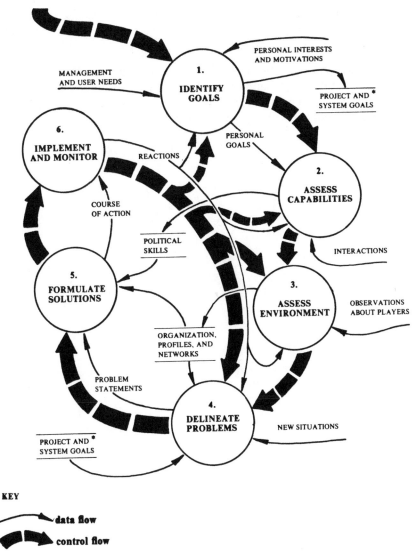

Figure 6.1. The six steps of the political process.

Chapter 6: Exercises

1. We have already seen two points in this book at which pieces of
    the political process can be observed: the actions of Stone and
    Mandel on the SCRIMP project, and in the evaluation described
    in Chapter 4. Each is an incomplete sample of the process, but
    both contain some very essential ingredients. Review these sec-
    tions and identify the elements of the process. Which elements
    are there and which elements are missing?

2. Consider the political interactions you have had. Begin with your
    most recent projects and proceed backward in time until you recall
    a situation in which you had political interactions. How did your
    process compare with the six steps introduced in this chapter?

7

IDENTIFYING GOALS

If you are without a clear understanding of what is being asked of you and are without an equally clear understanding of what you are trying to do, any political action you take is potentially misdirected. For whatever reasons, if you are trying to achieve some end that is not what management wants, then success becomes failure — that is, being politically successful in redirecting events toward your ends may in fact move the situation away from the actual goals. More probably, a misunderstanding of goals will lead to the escalation of political battles, until it becomes clear to everyone that you are not doing what is needed. An example is the manager who continues to build a high technology system while the company, hard pressed by severe cash flow problems, seeks a solution having minimum development costs. The project manager, not recognizing the company's financial dilemma, continues to propose system solutions that are too costly, until finally the effort is canceled or someone more attuned to management's need is asked to lead it.

While understanding goals might seem to be simply a matter of paying attention, my experience is that the signals from management frequently are unclear, and that project managers often are unable or unwilling to hear the signals, due to their own personal goals. This second point, the inability or unwillingness of project managers to hear the goals, involves personal motivations. I have known project managers who appear to be trying to self-destruct by ignoring direct inputs from management and plowing ahead, and project managers who seem incapable of any movement toward building the system. These problems are potentially fatal to both the project and the manager, and while they are difficult and sometimes touchy issues, their consequences demand that we deal with them.

In this chapter, we will consider both types of goals: the goals of the system and project as defined by management, and the goals of the project manager.

7.1 System and project goals

The fundamental questions when considering system and project goals are, What is being asked of the project team? What system is requested and what constraints and limitations are placed on the system and the system builders?

In Chapter 4, we discussed understanding the goals and constraints of the project and system as part of the process of taking control of a project. The process discussed here considers the same issues, but in more depth. We need to know the functions to be implemented; the existing systems and procedures to be replaced; the operational and environmental constraints on the system; the constraints on the project (such as time, resource, or budget limits); and specific requirements for automation (such as an integrated database, distributed network, specific terminals, interactive online updating, or software packages). In Chapter 4, the emphasis was on analyzing the feasibility of the project and deciding whether to accept the job. Here, we assume that the job is yours and the system and project goals and constraints are real. They need either to be accepted or, if they are not reasonable, somehow to be changed. But the first order of business is to understand what they are.

Projects are commissioned to build systems. And the systems are built for users, possibly including formal customers and surrogate users. These users, represented by user management (as defined in Chapter 3), are the primary source of information about system goals and constraints and, to a certain extent, project constraints. Direct management (as defined in Chapter 3) may be another source of information, about budget and resource limitations in particular, but also about additional constraints, functional requirements, or automation limitations of the system.

Use Table 4.1 in Chapter 4 as a checklist of categories of goals and constraints. Look for the information in various memos and reports, formal system request documents, or possibly a system charter. It may be necessary to ask user management and your direct management to clarify the goals and constraints as explicitly as possible.

The project manager must understand three points: what has been requested, what is expected, and what is most important. This last point, what is most important, is critical. In all probability, all the goals and constraints are serious and are expected to be met. But when it becomes apparent that all the goals and constraints cannot be met, some will emerge as vital, while others will be of lesser importance.

For example, several years ago a very large project team was assigned to build a system central to the function of its company. Project management was asked to build the very best system of its kind in the industry and to have it operational within three years. Because no one had implemented a system as large and complex as the one requested, the project team began building its new, technically advanced system with the knowledge that it would not be easy, but also with enthusiasm for the new path that would be cut. It soon became clear to team members that, due to the state-of-the-art nature of the new system, the three-year time frame would not be met. After two years of development, project management announced a six-month slip. Soon, the project slipped another six months, and another, and still another. By the time the project had slipped another six months, management had lost confidence in the project team, canceled the entire effort, and set up another project team in a different city to build a system as soon as possible. The fallout from the aborted effort was great, with many firings and demotions.

The central issue in this sad story is a misunderstanding of goals. Project management had heard that the team must build the best system of its kind in the industry, with three years as a target date. Corporate management wanted the best system of its kind, but very much needed the system within three years, since its old system was obsolete, preventing the company from being competitive. Project management did not understand the critical nature of the three-year goal, even though it fully understood that, since it was breaking new technological ground, there would probably be significant delays. If corporate management had been presented with the difficulty of meeting the three-year deadline, it certainly would have settled for less system to make its time goal (that's what it ended up getting anyway), particularly if told that such a system could be upgraded over time to ultimately meet the original goals. But having failed to understand the corporation's real priorities, project management proceeded with no warning to corporate management, and the project and its system failed with serious consequences for both the company and the project managers.

Project management in this story failed to understand priorities, partly because it did not ask, and partly because it did not appreciate the corporation's reasons for building the new system. Rather, the project managers were caught up in their own excitement of building a state-of-the-art system, and simply assumed that corporate management would understand the delays. If project management had taken the corporate perspective, and understood why the team had been commissioned to build the new system, it would have realized that the three-year time frame was a crucial goal.

A lesson from this story is that in order to understand what is really important to management, it is advisable to understand why the system has been requested as well as the motives behind that request. Examples of typical reasons for building systems follow:

- to meet a requirement by an outside agency or law
- to meet competition
- to support a customer request
- to support another system
- to support a new user process
- to replace a system that has excessive operating costs
- to introduce new technology

Some reasons, such as meeting competition or complying with legal requirements, will dictate time as a critical goal. Others, such as supporting new user processes, may dictate function as most critical. Still others, such as the desire for new technology, may demand a specific type of automation. By definition, critical goals cannot be compromised.

The reasons given in the previous paragraph are relatively simple. People are typically motivated by more than one reason; and so, you must understand the combinations and their implications for the project and system.

Identifying system and project goals involves understanding and documenting the specific goals and constraints of the system and project. Sources of this information include any available project documents, reports, and memos, and meetings with both user and direct management. When you think you've correctly identified them, present the goals and constraints to user and direct management for review and approval (some sort of formal sign-off). In some organizations, this process is an early step in the system building methodology and results in the document called the project charter. Charter approval is a go/no-go decision point for the project.

As the story of the ill-fated state-of-the-art system illustrates, it is not enough to know the detailed goals and constraints. You also need to look closely at management's reasons for requesting the system, and to make sure you understand them. With this understanding, identify the critical goals and constraints, those that are most important to users and management. Make sure the project will not compromise these critical items. This second part of the process is much less formal and is difficult to verify. You can't ask management which goals they are willing to give up. They won't tell you, and may not even know until the heat is on and they realize that some goals will have to give.

7.2 Personal goals

In the above story in which project management misread the corporation's need for a system in three years, other issues were involved. When the project team was commissioned to build the best system of its kind in the industry, no one had ever built a system of that size and complexity. Consequently, the project team would be pushing back the frontiers of system development. This was exciting to both project management and to all the members of the project team, much more exciting than simply building a system of reduced complexity in a three-year time frame. Team members had visions of papers presented at conferences, articles published in periodicals, and books written. In short, their visions of fame, recognition, and glory became as important to the team members as the other goals of the project.

The project leaders did not perceive the importance of the three-year time frame partly because they did not want to. Project management wanted to push back the frontier, to build the state-of-the-art system at whatever cost − and when the corporation asked for it, no one wanted to argue against it. In this case, personal goals got in the way of project success, and the consequences were fatal to the project and detrimental to the careers of the project leaders.

The consequences of conflicting personal goals are not always fatal. Much depends on how far the project team wanders from the corporate goal, how critical the project is to the organization, how visible it is, and how much money is at stake. But the point is made: If the personal motivations of the project manager prevent understanding of and conforming to the system and project goals, the project team will proceed in a different direction than is desired. This usually results in the project team's trying to build the wrong system, and eventually in some sort of confrontation with corporate management.

As another example, in a company whose primary business was supplying hardware and supporting software for high technology government contracts, a project manager was asked to build the process control support for a weapons system. The weapons system was to be sold by the United States government to a third-world nation whose political leanings and motivations the project manager questioned. The project manager reluctantly agreed to take the assignment because he felt it was necessary for his career. During the course of the project, he discovered that the government-specified requirements appeared to be incorrect in such a way that the weapons system would not function correctly under certain critical conditions. After much agonizing thought, he elected to say nothing. He was not certain of his conclusions, but hoped he was right. He believed that he could safely ignore the issue and that fingers would be pointed at the government specifications if and when the problem was discovered.

In this example, we have a person at odds with his principles, and the dilemma affected his management of the project. It does not matter whether his opinion about the specifications was correct; the project manager was engaged in passive sabotage of his own project and system. If he questioned the morality of his job, he should have refused the assignment rather than allow failure to be built into the weapons system.

In both this example and the previous one, the project manager's personal goals were different from the project and system goals. In both cases, the motivations were understandable and relatively easy to identify. If a friend had asked, "Is it important that the system be state of the art?" or, "Are you questioning the morality of selling this weapons system to that country?" it would have been reasonable to answer yes. Neither position would be considered shameful or embarrassing. In looking into personal goals and motivations, this is not always the case.

The examination of goals and motives involves an introspective process. It requires you to look at what makes you tick, not just on the job, but in your life. It requires that you look at yourself deep inside, and that you try to understand what you are really trying to achieve. You may not like what you find, and you may not be willing to share it with anyone, nor even to admit it to yourself.

We will first examine this area by discussion. The discussion may help you to discover some of your own motives, but only if they are already reasonably close to the surface. After the discussion, I will suggest some techniques that you can use to try to discover deeper motivations. These techniques may cause you some discomfort, but since no one else need be involved, at least give them a try.

7.3 Discovering personal motives

Most of us have motivations on our job that have little to do with the actual assignments we are given, motivations that relate to the kind of personal interaction we need or the roles we like to fill. In some cases, these motivations are totally congruent with doing a good job, and so no conflict arises. In other cases, the motivations are at cross-purposes with the job, and we experience conflict. Usually these motivations are held in check by feelings of responsibility to the job and by the awareness that others are watching . . . but sometimes they are not.

A few examples may be helpful. What follows are some possible motivations and their potential impact on a project. The list is far from complete, but should stimulate understanding of your motivations.

- [ ] *Fear of failure* — Since you might fail, you are afraid to do anything. You decide to do nothing and consequently fail. A related problem is the fear of breaking any rules and the resultant need to follow rules no matter what. If you follow the rules, you can blame the rule-maker.

- [ ] *Need for vengeance* — Every chance you get, you take a cheap shot at a specific individual, a department, or possibly the company for which you work. You may even destroy the project and yourself to hurt the object of the vengeance.

- [ ] *Desire for popularity* — You want everyone to like you and will do nothing that might be judged unpopular. So, you avoid any difficult decisions, including those needed by the project.

- [ ] *Fear of responsibility* — You just want to play, and regard the computer as a toy. It's more fun to do clever things than to implement the system. It's also not as scary.

- [ ] *Dislike of job* — You hate your job and want out. You avoid doing any of the things you dislike until you finally are doing nothing, and perhaps are hiding.

- [ ] *Self-glorification* — You want everyone to know how good you are. This need for oohs and aahs may get in the way of doing less visible but necessary activities, and may generate resentment by team members and others with whom you work.

☐ *Ambition* — You want a promotion, a raise, power, or more status. If you perceive that building a successful system will get you these things, there is no problem; but you may see other approaches that amount to your looking good at the expense of the project or other people.

☐ *Criticism* — You like to criticize people, especially those dumb, uptight, compromising managers. This adolescent sniping at authority is very common among programmers and has a self-righteous quality to it. Superficially, it may be idealistic, but underneath the message is, "You're stupid and awful." This constant criticism or finding fault makes enemies of people who are probably in a position to do you and your project harm.

☐ *Complaining* — Every chance you get, you complain about how awful things are with someone who also likes to complain. The more time you spend complaining, the less time you spend working. Anyway, if things ever got better, you couldn't complain anymore.

☐ *Martyrdom* — You find ways to carry the burdens of the world and honorably fail because of the deeds of others and because of unfair circumstances. As a reward, people feel guilt and pity for you. You may not even notice the project burning behind you.

I think you get the idea. These are personal, usually hidden, motives. We all have some of them or others like them. In most of us, they remain hidden and do no harm. In others, they are active, but still not consciously recognized.

Look inside yourself and discover your own motives. Do you truly want to build a successful system or are you afraid of failing, trying to avenge someone, acting disinterested, trying to get promoted, blaming others, looking for sympathy, avoiding problems, trying to look good or smart or to be a bigshot, and so on. Everyone's motivations are personal, and it's up to you to try to understand yours. You can do this privately with no one else involved, or you could ask the opinion of someone you trust, someone who might provide some interesting insight.

7.4 Origin of motivations

At a basic level, every one of us has a way of behaving, a way of responding that is unique to, and determined by, our particular needs. Most of these responses were formed when we were young as a result of our seeking a way to interact with parents or other significant adults who would satisfy our needs for social contact and survival. In other words, as children we interact by trial and error until we get the responses we desire. For the rest of our lives, we spend time and energy setting up similar situations that will generate the same type of familiar and comfortable responses, making us feel the same sense of security we had as children. Wanting to be liked, shutting down in the face of difficult decisions, and being critical may all result from childhood conditioning.

Some of these responses are good and help us live successfully and happily; others are not overly significant; and still others can be destructive to us and people around us, with potentially drastic personal consequences. In any case, these behaviors and their motivations tend to be outside of our awareness, and they are often manipulative in that we use them to force people to give the responses we are seeking.

Although our behavior patterns are automatic, they can be changed.* However, they are so ingrained that the change takes time and practice.

7.5 Beyond discussion

I indicated that we would discuss personal goals and motivations and would then explore other ways of gaining insight into them. The exercises listed below are designed to do this, but before we start them, several things need to be noted: First, if you dislike the exercises or feel uncomfortable doing them, don't do them. Either read through them to get an idea of what is involved, or simply skip them. Second,

---

*Here, we are delving into human psychology, and I make no claim to being a psychologist. Much of psychology is directed at exploring manipulative behavior, and one school that discusses it in terms that are generally understandable to laymen is Transactional Analysis. The TA term for manipulative behavior is Game. Rather than overstep my area of competence, I recommend reading Dr. Eric Berne's bestseller of the sixties, *Games People Play* (New York: Grove Press, 1964). This book and others like it can help you explore your motivations not only on the job, but in all situations, at a level far beyond what we will discuss in this book.

all of us have the behavior patterns described in the preceding section or, in Dr. Eric Berne's terms, all of us engage in games, so you are not alone. The challenge is to discover which ones you engage in, and then work on ways to change.

Third, if you are using these exercises to help gain insight, don't just read through them, do them as suggested. And don't go on to the next exercise until you've completed each step of the one you're on. In fact, cover the description of the next exercise so that you won't be distracted. Finally, to do the exercises, find a quiet place where you won't be disturbed and set aside five to fifteen minutes for each one.

Chapter 7: Exercises

Take a pencil and paper. Before starting, sit quietly for a moment and let other issues and thoughts settle down . . . then begin:

1. Review the list of possible motivations given in Section 7.3 (fear of failure, need for vengeance, and so on). Make your own list of motivations that you have observed in people in your work environment. If you feel that any items on my list are misstated, change them so they match your personal experience. When you are satisfied that your list fits your observations, go on to exercise 2.

2. Select three or four people from your work environment; ideally, they should be managers. They may be people whom you like or dislike. Place each person's name alongside each motivation from the list in exercise 1 that seems to fit his or her behavior. Expand the list to include other motivations any of these people might have. Find at least one person you know who fits each category.

3. Consider your current or most recent assignment. Make a list of significant interactions you had or managerial decisions you made that involved other people (exclude decisions that were purely technical). On the left side of the page, record what actually happened in these situations. On the right side, indicate what you wanted to happen. If what actually happened was different from what you wanted, ask yourself if your actions helped cause the end result. Could it be that part of you really wanted what actually happened?

4. List the situations in your work environment that create any intense emotional response, such as anger, sadness, tension, or fear ("Every time Jack does this, I want to . . ."). Even thinking about some of these situations may cause a physical reaction, such as tight muscles, queasiness, shaky hands, perspiration, or a red face. These reactions and the situations that generate them, particularly those that happen frequently, are clues to some of your motivations. Try to understand what disturbs you about these situations and how your reactions affect your job performance.

5. Return to the list you used in exercise 2. Consider each item carefully and place your name alongside the motivations that fit. Again, expand the list if necessary.

6.   On a piece of paper, draw a large circle. Make a pie chart in which each wedge represents the percentage of the time you have each of the motivations listed in exercise 5. Make sure you include a slice that represents the portion of time during which you are acting responsibly and doing your job the way you think it should be done.

7.   As the final exercise, make a list of all your personal motivations that get in the way of your acting responsibly in your job. For each one, write down the circumstances that usually lead to problems. Now write down at least two things you can do to control your actions in each kind of situation.

If you have conscientiously done each of these exercises, by now you probably have considerable insight into your nonconscious motivations. Just recognizing them makes them easier to control. To further the process of controlling your behavior and changing your responses, you will need to catch yourself as they are happening. Be patient; you've had years of practice mastering these actions, so it may take some time to control and change them.

8

ASSESSING YOUR CAPABILITIES

If you talk to athletes or to their coaches about winning, one item they always stress is fundamentals. The baseball manager can plan the most sophisticated strategies to no avail if his players can't hit the ball or can't catch it. The football team will lose if the linemen can't block, the defense can't tackle, the quarterback can't throw, and the running backs fumble.

In all fields, it's necessary to be good at fundamentals. The guitar player who can't hold a chord or the pianist with poor fingering will not play well. In short, if you don't have the basic skills, you might as well fold your tent and go home. If a manager is to thrive in the political arena, he must know the fundamentals of politics. Since politics consists mainly of interacting with other people, those fundamentals are the ways of interacting.

Assessing your capabilities means evaluating the tools you have: what they are, how good they are, and how well you use them. If a baseball team has speed, the players bunt, hit, run, and steal bases. If they have power, they swing for the fences. In order to succeed in politics, you must understand your capabilities and use them to your advantage, and you need to work on the tools you don't use very well.

In this chapter, we examine your capabilities. We will look at the various ways of interacting and how good you are at them. The result of this assessment will be an inventory of things you do well and things you don't do so well, and a better understanding of the way you use these fundamental skills.

8.1 A lesson

Several years ago, I was a member of a project team whose goal was to identify the major computer applications needed by our corporate division. The effort was to last a year and was staffed by me and other members of our division, along with an equal number of people from one of the major computer vendors. The vendor's goal was to help us find applications, in hopes that we would need and buy more of its hardware. The vendor was serious enough about the effort to supply project team members and the project manager at no cost.

A few months into the project, we were making reasonable progress and recognized that it was time to report to management, in this case a steering committee composed of the four vice-presidents of our division. Our project manager, realizing that management would react more positively if one of their own presented the report, gave me the lion's share of the assignment. We spent several days preparing numerous overhead projector foils detailing our activities, and when the meeting began, the project manager quickly passed the ball to me. Twenty minutes into the presentation, one of the vice-presidents excused himself, saying he had an important call to make but that he would try to return. Fifteen minutes later, a second vice-president left for some other reason. As we neared the fifty-five minute mark, the third vice-president departed; and when the last one left ten minutes later, I looked around at the remaining group − all of whom had helped put the presentation together − dropped my pointer, uttered an all-encompassing obscenity, and sat down.

This was certainly one of the low points of my career. The next morning I met with my boss (who had also attended the meeting) and discussed the disaster. We concluded that the presentation had been much too long and detailed, that I needed to learn a great deal about making presentations, and that the project manager was a nitwit. Any manager who had the poor judgment to turn a meeting over to a completely inexperienced presenter with no practice session did not understand the fundamentals of management presentations, and was himself either inexperienced or a nitwit. This project manager was experienced.

I survived the disaster — the project manager did not. Two weeks later, the vendor quietly replaced him with a politically more astute fellow, who gave all future presentations himself.

The lesson to be learned here is that, even though the project team was doing a reasonably good job, we managed to put our worst foot forward, boring management and leaving its members uninformed about what we were doing and unimpressed with our ability to represent management's best interests. My speaking ability at the time was certainly not my best political skill; and a ninety-minute detailed presentation was not what the vice-presidents needed, wanted, or expected. We were lucky to survive, luckier than the project manager.

8.2 Understanding interaction

In any kind of political interaction, you need to use your best tools, not your least effective ones. In order to do that, you need to identify your tools and assess your use of them. To help you, I've listed the most common types of interactions in Table 8.1.

Table 8.1
Common Interaction Categories

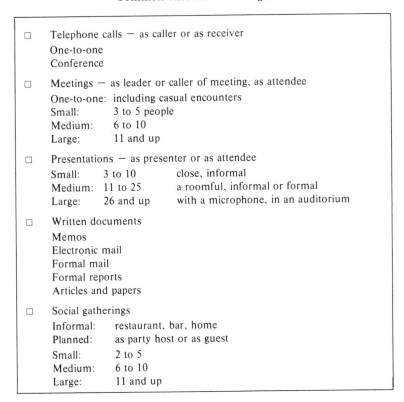

☐ Telephone calls — as caller or as receiver
One-to-one
Conference

☐ Meetings — as leader or caller of meeting, as attendee
One-to-one: including casual encounters
Small: 3 to 5 people
Medium: 6 to 10
Large: 11 and up

☐ Presentations — as presenter or as attendee
Small: 3 to 10   close, informal
Medium: 11 to 25   a roomful, informal or formal
Large: 26 and up   with a microphone, in an auditorium

☐ Written documents
Memos
Electronic mail
Formal mail
Formal reports
Articles and papers

☐ Social gatherings
Informal: restaurant, bar, home
Planned: as party host or as guest
Small: 2 to 5
Medium: 6 to 10
Large: 11 and up

Each category of interaction has a multitude of variations and potential pitfalls. Understand them all well enough to evaluate how you perform in each category. The subcategories are significant. For example, meetings you call with peers or non-managerial users are very different from meetings called by your steering committee or the top user manager. Your skill probably will vary depending on the subcategories. The characteristics and some of the variations of the categories in Table 8.1 are discussed in the following paragraphs.

8.2.1 Telephone calls

The *telephone* is a constant companion to everyone in the business world. In most offices, a phone call usually initiates all contact. For people separated by distances, it may be the only contact for long periods of time.

Lack of visual contact is the primary characteristic of the one-to-one phone call. Consequently, all nonverbal messages need to be conveyed by voice intonation. Subtle messages, such as attempts at humor, can easily be misconstrued; and when one person is unable to see the other's reaction, the misunderstanding may go undetected. The caller has the advantage of having planned what to say, while the receiver may be caught off guard and must be constantly alert. Either party can terminate a phone call much easier than a face-to-face meeting by "being called away" or "having a meeting." Consider how well you handle phone calls to peers, bosses, and others, including calls to people you have never met.

The conference call is a quasi meeting; it is normally used when people are unable to meet face to face. It's difficult to use, because telephone conversations among multiple participants generally are plagued by many interruptions and false starts. You need to be very good at conference calls if your conference deals with serious issues or problems.

8.2.2 Meetings

The *meeting* is the most common interaction in the business world, and it comes in all sizes and forms. There are one-to-one, small, medium-sized, and large meetings, each with its own level of formality. The one-to-one meeting is considerably different from larger meetings. It takes on a personal, sometimes secret air, and gives the feeling of unilateral decisions being made and backroom power conferred. Included in one-to-one sessions are casual encounters in the halls, cafeteria, and so on. Although these meetings are unplanned, they can often be very useful.

Some of the reasons for meetings are to negotiate, to lobby, to identify and solve problems, to review products, to deal with routine formalities (regular briefings and rubber stamp meetings), to give information, to confront, to make decisions, and to establish blame. As an added complication, your role is different depending on whether you call the meeting, lead it, or simply attend.

Consider how you perform in each type of meeting, both as leader and as participant, and take into account the size of the meeting. Ask yourself if you have any bad habits or if you sometimes do things that seem to annoy other people. A friend of mine does well in most meetings, but in medium-sized groups of peers and bosses, he gets very military in his bearing, and is often perceived as giving orders. This habit irritates many people, and is at best tolerated by others. Another friend of mine is fine one to one or in small groups, but takes a back seat in larger groups, and rarely expresses his opinion or gets what he needs from these sessions. A third can't resist the urge to argue, especially in medium-sized sessions, and likes to take control, even if he is clearly not the leader.

The meetings that are of particular importance politically include negotiations, lobbying efforts, confrontations, decision-making meetings, and meetings to establish blame. Rate your performance in these types of sessions carefully.

8.2.3 Presentations

Presentations are probably the most misused of all the categories of interaction. Although the presenter has the opportunity to convey a message without interference, the opportunity often is lost (as with my disaster story). Reasons for presentations include to give status reports, to request approval and funding, to convey information, to teach and train, to sell, and to give routine briefings. They come in all sizes, from three people participating, to roomfuls, to filled auditoriums. The presenter can find himself in a conference room, in the boardroom, or on the rubber-chicken circuit.

The primary distinguishing characteristic of presentations is the type of visual aid, ranging from none to blackboards, flip charts, overhead projection foils, thirty-five millimeter slides, movies, and videotapes. Success of the presentation depends on the presenter's delivery, the quality of the visuals, and the fit between the material and the audience. Because the presenter is in control, this can be one of the most effective types of interaction; but it is important not to venture to the podium unless you know what you are doing.

8.2.4 Written documents

People who enter technical fields, such as data processing, frequently don't appreciate the importance of *written documents*. In their schooling, such people totally avoided any class that required written papers. As testimony to most people's inability to write, the newspapers regularly feature "ain't that awful" articles about why Johnny can't write above sixth-grade level, even after getting his degree. If you are one of these people, and cannot express yourself in writing, your future as a manager is in jeopardy.

In this category of written communication, I include memos, formal reports, articles for publication, and electronic mail. For all these documents, good grammar, as well as correct spelling, is important. And most important is clarity of expression.

Memos are by far the most common of the written documents, although over the next few years electronic mail may surpass them. A memo can be thought out, drafted, typed, and reviewed before it is sent. But people are often trapped by their selection of words, and aren't always able to compose sentences that say exactly what they mean. (In contrast, the trial-and-error nature of vocal contact is more accurate. You can keep revising what you just said by a series of "I means" until the message has the right meaning.) Because the memo involves no visual or vocal contact, people write things that they would not say in person. Also, memos give no feedback, making them even trickier than phone calls. As an added disadvantage, they are a written record of what you said — so be careful.

Electronic mail, the new kid on the block, has a strange characteristic of pseudospontaneity. Unlike a memo, electronic mail encourages the tendency to "write from the hip" as if you were talking directly to the person. There is less planning, and so a greater possibility of saying something you did not mean. On the other hand, you can easily correct what you wrote with a second transmission. The trend is to use electronic mail as a replacement for phone calls (saving time by avoiding no answers and busy signals) and as a replacement for memos (saving clerical time and delays caused by external delivery). If electronic mail is used to replace phone calls, beware that it is less personal than either face-to-face or phone contact, and can lead to animosity at either end, since the mood and context of the message is easily lost without visual or audio contact. If electronic mail is used to replace memos, plan first and perhaps make a draft of what you want to say.

Formal reports differ from these other written forms of communication in that they are longer, usually printed and distributed to a relatively large audience, and often are intended to serve as ongoing references. Included here are specifications, the vital communications link of most DP projects. For openers, formal reports should meet the standards of the organization. Most important, they should be suited to their audience. Middle- and upper-level managers are not normally interested in technical detail, and generally will not read a detailed document, while analysts and programmers need the detail, finding summaries and overviews suitable only as introductions.

Some reasonable rules of report writing are to include an abstract and a summary of findings, followed by background, specific findings, and supporting detail. This format allows people with varying interests and knowledge to read as far as needed into the document. Specifications normally have some skeletal standards naming what sections are to be included. But again, as a suggested rule, a summary, background, and narrative are useful introductions, along with reasonable support data such as a glossary. Understand your audiences and tailor the document to their collective needs.

Formal reports can be big political guns, especially when prepared by outside groups such as consultants or auditors. They have an air of officiality and objectivity, and, if well written for the right audience, can have great impact on a political situation.

Articles for publication, including books, can also be political tools. A published article has much more impact than a mere internal report, even if written by a member of the project team. More common is the use of articles or books written by others as references to validate a point of view. Published documents need to attract and keep the interest of a generally much broader audience than internal reports; and they must clearly explain the subject to the intended audience, since the authors are usually not available to answer questions.

Evaluate your skills in using each of these written documents. Consider your grammar, clarity of expression, ability to convey your message, and how well you understand what the audience needs.

8.2.5 Social gatherings

Although not often thought of as political, *social gatherings* often are of primary importance in political interactions. Outside the office the rules change; people are less guarded, and often much less rigid in their behavior (a manager who may feel the need to conform in the office can relax after work in the local lounge).

Social gatherings are really another form of meeting, and your role changes based on the type of gathering and on whether you are host or guest. In controlled gatherings such as small dinner parties or lunch groups, much can be accomplished in terms of building and reinforcing networks of alliances and friendships. Often, minds can be changed and agreements reached more easily over coq au vin and a good chardonnay than in the office.

The social gathering often includes spouses and partners, and the behavior of people tends to change when their partners are present, usually for the better. Many times, I have observed that relatively mean and unpleasant people have delightful spouses, and interact much more willingly and decently when they are around.

In addition to being potentially productive, social gatherings, particularly parties of various sorts, are also potentially destructive. We often find ourselves with people from other countries or from other subcultures within our society. In either case, there is a chance you may offend a person from another culture with behavior that is entirely reasonable within your cultural group. In addition, the use of alcohol and other behavior-altering substances makes for possible disaster if you lose control (spilling your fifth Scotch on your most important user's wife as you trip over his newly acquired sixteenth-century Chinese vase is not the most endearing of actions).

As with any face-to-face interaction, evaluate your habits and characteristics in social gatherings. Do some people get offended, or are you normally the most sought-after person at the party? How effective are you in the various social settings at establishing and building your network, at changing minds, and at reaching agreements?

8.3 Summary

Use the checklist in Table 8.1 in combination with the preceding discussion to gain insight into your own types of interaction. Evaluate your performance in each of these areas in terms of your effectiveness and your predisposition to use them. Your evaluation will tell you which interactions to use, which to avoid, and which need practice. Pay attention to what you do in the various interactions and keep updating your evaluation and improving your use of these skills.

Finally, as with Chapter 7, this chapter is primarily introspective in nature. It's fine to read the words, but the main benefit comes from actually doing the exercises. The exercises on the following page enable you to examine your specific abilities. Read them and take some time to examine your skills as they suggest.

Chapter 8: Exercises

1. Make a list of your most common interactions with the players from your current and most recent assignments, using the various subcategories in Table 8.1. If you have had interactions not identified in the table, add them to the list. Note the type of people involved (bosses, peers, and so on) and any circumstance that might make an interaction different from others in its sub-category. List at least ten interactions.

    Rate the interactions in terms of frequency, with the most frequently occurring interaction at the top of your list.

2. For each interaction on your list, identify at least three good and three bad characteristics that you exhibit. Keep in mind that you are evaluating your interactions from a political viewpoint — being fun to be with at a party may not advance your situation politically. Try comparing yourself to other people who you believe perform well or poorly at each interaction. List what they do well and what they do poorly. If you have (or lack) similar characteristics or tend to have opposite characteristics, note them.

3. Now, evaluate yourself. Using Table 8.2 below as a guide, rate your performance in each interaction on the scale of 1 to 5. If you identify any additional good and bad points, add them to your list. If there are any ratings in the top five interactions on your list that fall below a 4, take note. You are not putting your best foot forward. These interactions should be avoided if possible, and you should work on eliminating your bad points. Any interactions rated 2 or 1 should not be used.

Table 8.2
Interaction Tool Evaluation Scale

RATING	MEANING
5	Terrific — smash hit. You are an expert at this type of interaction. Other people should watch you to learn how.
4	Definitely in your skill box. This tool works well for you. It can be used to interact successfully with other people.
3	This one needs some work, but it's still passable. You can use it once in a while, but don't count on it as your primary tool. If you like using it, get some training and practice.
2	Don't use this one. If you ask your friends how you did, they'll smile weakly and mumble something unintelligible. Practice and training may help, but for now, avoid it.
1	Forget it. Even your mother would groan and hide her head. If you want to make a sow's ear from a silk purse, this is the way.

9

ASSESSING
THE ENVIRONMENT

Our senses are continuously bombarded with input from the environment. To sort this input, we set up filters to separate relevant information from the massive onslaught of data. A mother responds to her baby's cry but is undisturbed by much louder noises; a driver notices slight changes in the movement of other cars nearby but is unaware of billboards; a worker in an office concentrates on an important task but doesn't hear the conversations around him. Some input enters the foreground of our awareness, while the vast majority is relegated to the background. Other inputs interrupt our actions, instantly bringing new and more important issues to the foreground. A swerving car causes a driver to brake almost before he is aware of any problem; a shift in the announcer's tone of voice and volume signals the sports fan to stop his conversation and listen to the game action.

While political events happen at a slower pace, the amount of data relating to them is still more than we can receive and interpret. Consequently, our filters selectively allow political information in, and our warning systems again interrupt only for certain events. Learning to assess the political environment can be viewed as modifying our filter and alert systems to be sensitive to the appropriate political inputs. This requires an understanding of what is relevant, and practice in paying attention to political inputs.

There are three areas to consider in assessing the political environment: the formal organization, the informal organization, and the players themselves. The formal organization represents the official delegation of authority and responsibility, and the official lines of communication. The informal organization represents the other interactions and lines of communication that exist among the various people in the organization: who talks to whom and who listens to whom. The players are the actors and reactors in both the formal and informal organizations, the producers of actions and changes. Relevant information about each of these areas needs to be extracted from the background noise.

9.1 The formal organization

In one project I led, for over a year I did not understand the formal mechanism for obtaining approval and funding. My lack of understanding resulted partially from the process being poorly and incompletely defined, but partially from my own disinterest in it. Fortunately, my immediate boss understood the process and was willing to hold my hand whenever a form or document needed to be submitted. The process was so complex that many people did not understand it, and in fact the administrators of the process used this complexity as a means of sabotaging projects they did not support.

Although the formal organization is usually the simplest part of the environment to understand, there are situations such as the above in which it is difficult to get a clear picture of responsibilities and of the processes required. In any case, they need to be understood. It is important to follow the proper processes so the process watchers do not become upset and cause trouble (process watchers are a subcategory of rule followers, a breed common to any large organization and the primary source of bureaucracy). It is also important to understand the formal responsibilities, to avoid inadvertently snubbing individuals who are supposed to be included.

The first step in understanding the formal organization is to draw a picture of it. This picture is called an organizational chart, and virtually every company of any size has one. It usually can be found in some official book of rules and regulations, and shows titles, formal reporting relationships (who works for whom), and, to a certain level, the names of the people holding titles. Not always included on these charts are various committees and structures that cross organizational boundaries: An example of one such committee is the SMC mentioned in the Smoot chapters. Such a group may be the most important portion of the formal organization, but since it is an overlay on the day-to-day organization, it may not appear on the charts. When drawing an organizational chart, be sure you do not overlook such committees and structures. Look as well for procedures that govern many of the activities in which your project is involved. These procedures exist, although possibly not in the same official book of rules and regulations.

Only a portion of the formal organization is relevant to a project. In large companies, even though the entire organization may be depicted in the charts, the relevant portion should be extracted, maintained separately, and understood. The understanding can be difficult, as the processes and organizational relationships in some companies are complex. Relevance can be judged by documenting the processes in which the project is involved and by listing the players (see Chapters 3 and 4).

Simply stated, to document the relevant formal organization, do these three tasks:

☐ From the list of players who interact with your project, identify their formal organizational slots.

☐ List all the processes the project needs to participate in, and carefully document the flow of information through the organization for each process, noting each organizational group or title involved.

☐ Document the formal organization surrounding all the groups and titles identified in steps 1 and 2. Draw the organizational chart and fill in the detailed structure beneath titles and inside the various groups. Describe the responsibilities and the structure of the groups. Extend the chart upward to encompass one or two reporting levels above each group or individual.

The exact format of the documentation is not critical. Some people prefer to describe responsibilities with words, while others prefer diagrams. You should collect enough information to understand how and when the individuals or groups interact with your project.

For example, if EDP auditors are involved in projects within your organization, you should know that the EDP auditors have a first-level manager and two grades of auditor, and report to the auditing department, which in turn reports to the corporate controller. You should also know under what circumstances they are involved in projects, what kind of interaction they have, what documents and other physical communications they require, and what authority they have over a project. The authority and responsibility of each manager should be understood.

Before you spend the rest of your career documenting the organization, take what I say with a grain of salt: You need to know enough about the people involved to find out about their organization before you interact with them. If the interaction is frequent, then you need detailed knowledge as I have suggested. If it is occasional, then a preliminary understanding is adequate for openers, but you will need to do your homework when the time comes to interact.

9.2 The informal organization: networks

In any organization, relationships between people exist that go beyond work requirements. These relationships may be the result of interaction on the job, affiliation in outside groups, mutual acquaintances, friendships, blood relationships, and so on, and can be current or historical (for example, attending the same school). The relationships are usually thought of as positive, but they can also be negative. These relationships compound the formal organization because of the influence one individual can have on another. In making decisions, we often seek the advice of those we know and respect, and we are swayed by the opinions of our friends and associates. Priorities can be shifted, rules bypassed, and roadblocks lifted when people we like are involved. Conversely, people whom we dislike or whose principles we disagree with can be thwarted or at least slowed by the reverse process.

Various kinds of relationships can exist within an organization depending on the relative positions of the individuals, their responsibilities, and their predisposition to interact with each other. I've listed some major ones below.

NEGATIVE RELATIONSHIPS:

☐ *Non-friends* — A dislike exists between the individuals; it can cause any or all work done for the other to be slowed, ignored, or rejected. The exact consequences depend on the authority of the individuals. Generally, nothing obviously harmful or illegal is done, but interactions are certainly made much more difficult.

☐ *Enemies* — An intense and active dislike or hatred exists between individuals, leading to attacks, vengeful acts, and conscious attempts to ruin the other. The power of the attacking individual depends on his authority and on his network of positive relationships (who can be influenced to act against the other). This warfare harms both parties, since the victim usually retaliates. An enemy relationship can be all-consuming.

☐ *Kid gloves* — Two individuals dislike but also respect each other. Both parties have enough maturity to control their feelings and treat each other ethically. Consequently, they feel like adversaries, but act properly and sometimes even give each other priority as a demonstration of proper conduct. Such a relationship is tenuous, but is the best that can be expected of people who dislike each other.

POSITIVE RELATIONSHIPS:

☐ *Influence* — A person with some authority and responsibility is influenced by the opinions of another. The other person is a confidant, and has access to this individual outside the formal organization. Person B can set or affect the policy and decisions that are person A's responsibility. Such a relationship may or may not be reciprocal.

☐ *Delegated authority* — Person A, in effect, delegates his authority to B, who makes all of the major decisions. This typically happens when A is either unsure or uninterested in his authority, particularly when B is eager to take it. Delegated authority is an extension of influence.

☐ *Allies* — Person B joins person A in A's struggle to do his job. Depending on B's position, this assistance can take the form of protection, support, or direct participation.

☐ *Information channel* — Person B is privy to secrets or at least to information from another organization, and shares the information with A. This is the mechanism of the rumor mill. B often is a clerical worker inside another organization (or, in popular spy jargon, a mole).

☐ *Patron/protégé* — Many people who reach the top do so with the help of someone who is already there, a patron. The patron latches on to the protégé as a sort of surrogate offspring, grooms him for future responsibility, and paves the way within his network for the protégé's promotion. The protégé supports and adopts his patron's philosophies, policies, and techniques.

☐ *Friends* — Friendship can exist without any of these other relationships, either because the friends feel some reluctance to deviate from the formal organizational structures, or because the need for or possibility of any assistance has not occurred. This is the most basic positive relationship, and I include within it any form of friendship or family relationship.

In each of these relationships, there are degrees. Friendships can range from strong to casual, allies may help only under certain circumstances, or information may be given only in specific areas. More than one relationship can exist between two people, and some relationships can exist between groups of people. While no doubt more relationships can be identified, those listed here cover most situations.

9.2.1 Your network

In assessing the informal organization, look first at your own network: It is the total of all the relationships you have in the organization, in whatever degree. In individual political situations, your network can be of importance in helping you win your point (or, if negative relationships are involved, hindering any specific effort). In the long term, your network is probably the single most important factor in your survival and advancement in the organization. Within it are your primary strengths, your friends, allies, sources of information, and potential benefactors.

The negative relationships can mean trouble, particularly if your adversaries hold positions of power. If you cannot somehow resolve the differences, then at least try to attain a kid-gloves relationship. Everyone has some redeeming value, and most of us can find some common ground of understanding with any person. Enemy relationships should be avoided; most enemies have a destructive impact on the careers and lives of their antagonists and themselves.

Nurture your positive relationships whenever possible. When trouble arises, your network will inform you, support you, and in some cases save you from serious difficulty. Make an effort to maintain and improve your network by continually contacting existing members. Expand it by reaching out to new people in the organization. While this may seem manipulative, reaching out to people whether they are already friends, allies, strangers, or possibly former non-friends is a positive step. Expanding and improving your network will not only help politically, but will also improve your overall interaction with people.

To document your network, simply code the various boxes on a copy of the organizational chart with the type of relationship you have with each individual. You might even color-code the boxes. Since not everyone is shown on the organizational charts, this is not a complete network and will have to be augmented. As an alternative, make a list of all the people you have relationships with, perhaps by location or group, and code the list with the type of relationship. Again, color may be used. This is more complete, but less graphic, than the previous suggestion.

Exactly how you document your network is not important, but it is important to identify it. You will find some surprises, both good and bad, and you may realize that some relationships have been neglected.

9.2.2 Other networks

Because of lack of information, you cannot fully understand anyone else's network. Consequently, casual and innocent comments and actions potentially can cause political damage. For example, while at lunch one day, you make a somewhat derogatory remark about a user. One of the secretaries at the table happens to belong to the user's church group, and has occasionally seen your user socially. The remark may not really have been intended, but only spoken out of frustration at some delay, and now it may make its way to your user, or influence the secretary not to support your team's activities as fully as possible.

From this example, two lessons can be extracted: Try to understand the networks of key players, particularly those with whom you do not have strong positive relationships, and don't say nasty things about people (such comments are usually rash and unreasonable, and they can come back to haunt you).

In spite of the difficulty of fully understanding other people's networks, simple observation and a bit of deductive reasoning can show you at least part of a network. Whenever you are in meetings with any of your players, keep your eyes and ears open for obvious negative or positive relationships. Tones of voice, body postures, and offhand comments are tipoffs to attitudes and feelings. Conversations with your friends and acquaintances can also provide information, especially in the form of gossip and rumors. Also, pay attention to various affiliations and histories. A long-time member of the organization has obviously worked with many other people along the way, and probably weathered storms with some and fought battles against others.

From this data, some relationships can be deduced and others presumed or suspected, and a set of networks, depicting some primary relationships, can be constructed. To represent other people's networks, use the same techniques you used for your own, or try to combine the data and draw an overall *influence diagram* showing major relationships between pairs of people overlaid on the organizational charts. This latter approach, illustrated in Fig. 9.1, is convenient and may be adequate for all the key network pairings.

In drawing these diagrams, you may feel intrusive. Some relationships are obvious to everyone, but documenting others can give you the sense of prying into someone else's secrets. Realize that this is an effective way of understanding who influences whom and in what way. The diagram is also a quick source of reminders for you when interacting politically or trying to figure out what happened and why. If you don't attempt to document relationships now, there will not be enough time available to get the information when you need it.

The informal organization of interest is represented by your own network and the networks of the various players who interact with you and your project. Your own network has far-reaching, long-term implications for your position in the organization, as well as being an immediate source of help or obstruction. The players' networks are key political structures that provide a more accurate view of why political events happen and what the players may do next.

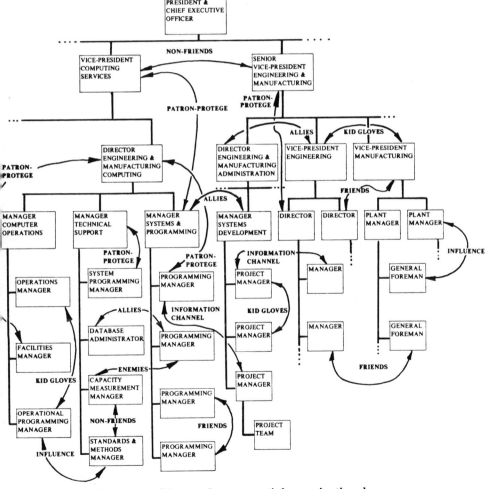

Figure 9.1. Blatzco, Inc. — partial organizational
influence diagram.

9.3 The players

At the nodes of the networks are the players. Since it is the players, governed by their own motivations, responsibilities, authorities, and predispositions, who cause the action, it is the players who ultimately must be understood.

Anyone who has even the slightest awareness of the political process and has participated in it has tried to understand at least some of the other participants. The effort to understand one's co-workers is clearly one of the most necessary activities in the political process. Unfortunately, it is also one of the most difficult.

To understand another player is to anticipate his reaction to circumstances, what he will do under a specific set of conditions. Stop for a moment and pick three of the players in your organization. When you have three in mind, ask yourself how each would respond if he discovered evidence that another of the players was guilty of stealing a thousand dollars' worth of company property? Would he confront the player? ignore the evidence? or send an anonymous letter to higher management? Or, would he use the evidence to pressure the player into giving him preferential treatment, or try the same thing himself?

You should have a guess for each of the three people. In making your guesses, you probably imagined each person confronted with the situation and intuitively concluded what that person would do. If you know each person well and have good insight, you might make some very good guesses. With less insight, the guesses become less reliable.

Anticipating someone's reaction to a given situation requires knowledge of the individual and an ability to use that knowledge to gain empathetic insight into how he will react. For people with whom you work regularly, you probably have the knowledge and can anticipate responses. But for people with whom you have only casual or infrequent contact, the prediction is quite difficult.

9.3.1 Governing factors

For anyone you wish to understand, make a conscious effort to gather relevant information about the factors that govern the individual's reactions to particular circumstances. For close associates, this will formalize what you already know, and will provide added insight and ability to anticipate their actions. For those people you do not know well, this exercise will cause you to pay attention to them, and should increase your understanding substantially.

Identifying relevant information is difficult. In my intuitive and formalized evaluation of people, I typically examine three areas: specific job responsibility and authority, goals and motivations, and the history of reactions to situations. In many cases, I have looked at exactly the kind of information suggested in Chapters 7 and 8, only instead of looking introspectively at myself, I looked externally at others.

☐ *Responsibility and authority:* These were discussed at some length in Chapter 4. Briefly, responsibility is what an individual's management expects him to do in and for the organization. Responsibility can be explicit — management has identified the goals and products it expects — or implicit. Implicit goals must be met to achieve success of the explicit responsibilities but are outside the individual's control. Authority is the individual's ability to affect the variables governing his responsibilities. To understand an individual, you must understand his responsibilities (what he must do well to be viewed favorably by his management), and his authority (what he is able to do within the organization).

☐ *Goals and motivations:* One likely goal of any individual is to meet his responsibilities. Other goals, as we saw in Chapter 7 in the discussion of personal goals, are not necessarily as obvious. In Chapter 7, the view was introspective, so the data was known (but not always consciously). In this case, the best we can do is observe and guess, and then correct our erroneous guesses as we gather more data.

Based on your observations and on any other evidence, take your best guess at the individual's goals in his current job. Next, try to understand his career goals, what he is working toward in the near and long term. Finally, consider his personal goals, values, and principles.

☐ *History of reactions to situations:* Evaluate the individual's use of the categories of interaction detailed in Chapter 8. Which ones does he use, and under what circumstances? Look in particular for interactions that may occur within your project. How has he reacted in the past to similar situations, and how successful was he?

This past behavior, along with your intuitive sense of the person's goals and motivations, provides the kind of data you normally use to judge what someone will do. We are formalizing the data collection, and consequently making it more correct, complete, and available.

9.3.2 Profiles

Formalize the process even further by preparing a profile of each person you evaluate. The profile should be a one-page summary, containing a set of one-liners describing the person in each of the categories listed in the preceding section. In addition to formal responsibility and authority, goals and motivations, and historical tendencies, be sure to include any specific facts that may be useful. Figures 9.2 and 9.3 contain sample profiles.

PROFILE

Joe Jones — Manager, Systems Development
Years with Blatzco, Inc.: 4
Age: 34

Responsibility and authority:

- Oversees all engineering and manufacturing applications development and maintenance
- Supervises 4 programming managers and 47 programmers and systems analysts

Goals and motivations:

- Is sensitive to budget and schedule
- Is primarily concerned with support of user
- Tends to let ongoing enhancements take priority over new development
- Wants to be director or vice-president of Computing Services
- Has alcoholic wife and personal drinking problem; two children
- Is a financial and political conservative
- Has never been in any job long enough to install any significant system or complete any major activity
- Is very conscious of his own image and appearance

Historical tendencies:

- Downgrades rivals to boss
- Assigns blame to others (peers or employees)
- Is quiet in meetings; prefers one-to-one lobbying in person or on telephone
- Rarely sends memos
- Does not confront problems directly with the person involved

---

Figure 9.2. Profile example.

PROFILE

Sam Smith — Capacity Measurements Manager
Years with Blatzco, Inc.: 12
Approximate age: 37

Responsibility and authority:
- Provides primary input for hardware and system software acquisitions and upgrades
- Supervises small staff (4 measurements analysts)
- Oversees special hardware measurement devices and software capacity simulation models

Goals and motivations:
- Protects computer from excessive capacity applications
- Has no apparent ambition for advancement
- Likes to show how smart he is
- Is socially a loner; divorced, lives alone
- Is athletic, very competitive at softball and tennis

Historical tendencies:
- Is quick to argue, especially in meetings
- Sends nasty memos
- Issues highly technical reports
- Blames most capacity problems on excessive user requirements
- Is very good at predicting system capacity
- Meets commitments once they are made

Figure 9.3. Profile example.

The initial development of profiles does not take long. All you need to do is sketch your impressions of each person, file them away, then observe. Over time, you will need to change the profiles, partly because of inaccuracies in your guesses, and partly because your perception of people may change, sometimes quite radically. In reviewing some of the assessments I've made, I wonder how I could have been so wrong. But then I realize that the available evidence led to those initial assessments, and that my current conclusions about the people were different from the original because the people or situation had changed.

To decide which profiles to prepare, start with the list of players involved with your project. Select from the list the players with whom you anticipate having the most critical and difficult interactions. Be sure to include anyone with whom you have had a negative relationship who has any current connection with you or your project.

This list of critical interactions and negative relationships is the minimum set of profiles I suggest. Add to the list any other players you feel are appropriate, and keep adjusting the list over time as people and situations change.

9.4 Summary

The steps outlined in this chapter are crucial to survival in a political environment. Begin the assessment with the formal organization, using organizational charts, job descriptions, and formal procedures as source documentation. If your organization is large or complex, extract the portion of the formal organization that is of interest to you and your project and maintain your own separate documentation.

Next in the assessment is the informal organization, the networks. First, document your own network, either by coding the relationships on the organizational charts or by preparing a coded list of all your network members. Then, prepare network information for all players involved with your project. The information may be limited, but do the best you can and continue to update the networks as you learn more. You might choose to draw an overall influence diagram, depicting the most significant network couplings, probably in the form of a modified organizational chart.

Finally, prepare individual profiles of the most crucial players and of your negative network relationships. As with the networks, these profiles should be updated periodically to reflect your current observations.

I suggest that this set of documents, which constitutes your assessment, be kept private. This will allow you to make comments or speculations without concern that other eyes will see them. They are nobody's business but your own.

Chapter 9: Exercises

1. Extract the formal organization of interest to the SCRIMP project from the charts and information already presented on Smoot. Build networks for Bernie Stone and R.A. Barnwell III, making some guesses as to likely relationships. Construct profiles for Stone, Fred Mandel, and Ralph Johnson.

2. Construct your network. Identify the relationships in the network most in need of attention and try to improve them.

3. Derive the formal organization of interest for your current or most recent project. Build an influence diagram or construct individual networks for the players. Prepare profiles for the five most crucial players.

10

DELINEATING PROBLEMS

For several weeks, my automobile has been vibrating at freeway speeds. Since the problem started, I've taken it to two different repair shops. Each time the car was apparently fixed, but both times the problem immediately returned, and now it is getting worse. During a weekend of driving several hundred shaking miles, I decided to take the car to the dealer first thing Monday morning.

At 7:30 a.m. Monday, the skies were very dark, the wind was howling, and the rain was pouring down. I called the dealer just before leaving the house. I told the service manager that I'd been having some front-end vibration and I wanted to bring the car in. "Not today," he said, somewhat tersely. "You'll need an appointment." After a moment he said, "We have room tomorrow. What's the name?"

"The name is Block," I said. "And by the way, I'll need a ride to my office, which is about three miles away."

"I'm sorry, we don't give rides," he said, again somewhat tersely.
"Well, what *do* you do?" I snapped.
"We fix cars," he shot back.
"Not mine," I replied in a hard voice. "I can't bring it in unless I get a ride!" I hung up with some vigor.

What's the problem here?

☐ The problem is he wouldn't give me a ride. How can he expect people to get their cars fixed if he leaves them stranded?

☐ The problem is my car is broken and for all I know the wheels are about to fall off. Nobody is able to fix it, and all I'm doing is spending money.

☐ The problem is it's Monday, it's raining, and I'm in a very bad mood.

☐ The problem is the service manager is a jerk. If he hadn't been so abrupt, I might not have hung up.

☐ The problem is I just made an enemy of the guy who has control of getting my car fixed. If I bring it in, he'll probably make sure it gets worse or charge me a bundle or both.

☐ The problem is I don't know anything about cars, so I have to rely on other people to fix them.

☐ The problem is our society has inadequate provision for getting around without a car.

While all of these comments identify some aspects of the situation that can be called a problem, none of the statements is particularly useful in proceeding to a solution. Each statement has an emotional quality to it that really has little to do with resolving the situation. Rather than identifying problems rationally, the statements assign blame and release emotional tension.

A more useful statement of the problem might be

☐ My car is broken and I have decided it needs to be repaired by the dealer. To do that, I need an appointment, a ride from the dealer's service center to my office in the morning and a return ride in the evening, and I need to make peace with the service manager.

This statement describes the problem and the solution environment in a rational, objective manner. It recognizes the situation for what it is rather than assigning blame. Achieving the identified situation may not in fact solve the basic problem of getting my car fixed, since the dealer's service department may not know how to fix it, but it is the best action I can think of right now. If this solution to the immediate problem does not work, I will have to reassess the situation and try again.

Before we discuss how to identify problems in a project environment, we must learn how to effectively formulate problem statements that are useful toward achieving solutions. In the example above, I stated that I needed to have the dealer's service department repair my car. This is a statement of the condition I wanted to have exist, which really was secondary to my true need to have my car not vibrate. The lack of an appointment, transportation, and a cooperative service manager were the immediate obstacles in the way of achieving the condition. Listing these needs provides an effective, useful problem statement, since satisfying these needs would cause the service department to (try to) repair my car.

This example can be generalized to form a reasonable definition:

problem   the difference between what is and what I
statement   would like it to be

Useful problem statements describe a condition that is desired but not yet achieved. By defining a problem in this way, we can begin formulating ways of reaching the desired situation — that is, we can begin determining solutions.

Even using this definition, we may state problems ineffectively: "I want public transportation to exist between my dealer and my office." While this statement defines a solution environment, achieving it is obviously unrealistic. On the other hand, if you overlook the capacity for human resourcefulness, you may exclude problem statements that seem to be unachievable, but really aren't.

Another characteristic of problem statements is that they are often solutions to higher-level problems. The need for a ride is contingent on my decision to have the dealer's service department repair the car, and the repair of the car is the higher-level problem. If the problem statement is unrealistic, as was the desire for public transportation, the problem can be raised to the next level of abstraction. In this case, the next level of abstraction is the need for a ride. The problem then could be restated to be more realistic, "I need to call a taxi." Problem identification, then, should result in the formulation of useful problem statements that exclude the ridiculous without precluding the possible.

10.1 Problem components

In a project environment, problems affect meeting the goals of the project, its system, the team members, and the project manager. Identifying problems, particularly the serious ones, is of fundamental importance to meeting these goals.

Problems can be identified by inspecting project products, or by examining the people involved in the projects. Since finding problems is so important, we will look at both approaches.

10.1.1 Products

Products include the external deliverables required of the project, products delivered to the team from subcontractors, reviews by internal and external groups, and formal approvals given by user and DP management. Each of these products may be the source of potential problems. Or, following our approach to problem statements discussed above, we can identify as problems any obstacles to producing or receiving high-quality deliverables that meet budget and schedule, or to passing reviews or receiving approvals.

For example, suppose your team is scheduled to produce the user requirements specification for a system within three months. The specification is to include functional descriptions of required processing, quantity and location of all remote terminal hardware, input and output user transaction volumes, and a cost estimate for the software development. In reviewing the situation, you estimate that five people are needed to complete the functional descriptions, but only three are available. You also note that no one is available to develop transaction volume data. Remote technical hardware requirements have been delegated to the user organization, but you are not confident that the job will be given to a competent person. Finally, you realize that reliable software estimates require understanding of the internal system design, which will not be completed for at least two months following delivery of your specification. Clearly, on-time delivery of the user requirements specification is in question.

Try to formulate a problem statement for the situation presented in the previous paragraph. In Chapter 5, Bernie, Marsha, and Steve did a similar analysis of SCRIMP and discovered several problems, not only with their ability to deliver the product, but also with the product itself as specified by LM&C.

So, look to the products. Consider each external deliverable, each subcontractor's product, each review, and each required approval. Identify the obstacles and from them formulate problem statements.

10.1.2 People

Problems with people are more difficult to identify. You must determine if any player involved with your project is adopting attitudes or opinions that could have an adverse impact on the project, system, project team, or project manager. These attitudes could result either from the player's own experiences and thoughts or from network inputs. Since we cannot read minds, it's difficult to know what problems exist with people.

In looking for problems, consider each player. Ask yourself if you are violating any protocol or procedure in which the player is involved, or if you are leaving the player uninvolved or excluded. Do you have a negative relationship with this player? Do you and the player potentially disagree over the approach to or content of the system or any product in which the player is involved? Next consider the player's network. What inputs could he be receiving from others that could affect his attitudes and opinions? Consider also the responsibilities and circumstances of the player's job. He may be forced into a position that is harmful to your project.

If the player is within your network of positive relationships, a rational possibility (particularly if you are unsure of a player's attitude or opinion) is to ask. In many cases, the actual problem results from lack of communication, so the asking in fact solves the problem. It would be naive to assume that everyone will tell you what he thinks, particularly if he suspects you won't like the answer; but some people will talk, and others will unintentionally give hints.

Your own network will be able to inform you about what is going on. Speak to anyone with whom you have an information channel relationship and any friend whose opinion as a nonparticipant might be more objective than your own.

Another source of information is the players themselves and their actions that are visible to you directly or through secondhand information. If you have done your homework, you already have profiles of the players. You can correlate their actions with your assessments in the profiles and then draw your conclusions about what is happening.

While all this may sound rather sterile, it is not. There is much emotion tied into looking for problems and to understanding what others are thinking and doing (or going to do). Usually, we lack information and don't pay attention (because we lack information, we don't believe a problem exists, so we look no further). We also have an inherent difficulty in understanding anyone else's thoughts, and a very human tendency to disbelieve bad news. Couple this with our inability to completely control the environment, even when we fully understand it, and we may feel so threatened that we lose perspective and act irrationally rather than in our own best interest.

Several years ago, I was managing a project that I thought was going well. A friend who was privy to information from one of the user organizations told me that the vice-president, my main management user, was growing disenchanted with the project and my performance. He was considering blocking approval of the project, and there had been discussion in his office of getting rid of me.

What I needed was a cold, calculated analysis of this very serious problem. Instead, my stomach tightened into knots, and I spent a lot of energy trying to rationalize why this information could not possibly be true. The potential for this kind of emotion is the best reason to make the analysis procedural. Force yourself to review each player in a disciplined manner. In your mind, disassociate yourself from involvement in your project and then evaluate what is going on. Try to see what's happening with the total objectivity of an outsider, almost as if the project were a play in progress.

Try to understand each player's motives and the environment in which he must live and operate. The key word here is empathy. If you can understand the player's perspective, you should be able to anticipate what he is likely to do. A successful technique for me involves first stripping myself of any emotional reaction, especially negative, to the person. Next, I try to imagine what it is like to be inside his skin, looking out through his eyes. I feel his responsibilities and pressures and possibly his world away from work. Then, I try to imagine how he will interact with me and my project.

If I am able to empathize, I gain new insight into a person — his current pressures, priorities, and state of mind, and his attitude toward me and my project. Or, if I'm unable to take on *his* persona, at least I'm able to understand what *I* would be feeling in his job. (This is often a reasonable approximation, but carries with it a dangerous assumption that he is motivated as I am. If this is not the case, then my ability to predict his attitudes and actions may be seriously hampered.)

10.2 Perceiving reality

A few years ago I met a good friend while in a local restaurant. We both had some time and had lunch together. I asked the friend how things were going. "Fine," he said, "the job's good, and the family couldn't be better." He went on to say that in these days of shattered families he was lucky to have such a good marriage. He and his wife were very close and felt terrible for all the couples they knew who had separated. I agreed, and said how pleased I was that things were going so well.

As you might have guessed, the next time I saw my friend, some six weeks later, he was ashen-faced, haggard, and visibly shaken. He said that a week after our previous meeting, his wife had told him that she was very unhappy and wanted to separate. After some intense conversations and several sessions with a marriage counselor, they did just that. Now he was on his own, living in a small furnished apartment until they could arrange a settlement. He shook his head and wondered aloud how he could have been so blind as not to see his wife's unhappiness.

Understanding what is happening inside someone else, even a spouse, requires information, energy, time, and an empathetic view of the person. In addition, it requires an ability to perceive reality as it is rather than as we would like it to be.

The techniques presented here provide ways for cracking through the multiple barriers to understanding our problems with people. Any one of us is simply not able to see all that goes on, what it means, and what's likely to happen. The challenge is to make a pragmatic, perceptive assessment of the reality surrounding us in spite of the obstacles, the most common (and the most solvable) of which is our own predisposition to deny bad news — the wishful thinking that it can't happen to me, even though it could to somebody else.

These techniques enable you to see reality as it is rather than the way you prefer it to be. Fundamentally, judging reality accurately requires painful honesty in self-evaluation. Beyond trying the suggested techniques, simply be aware of your own tendency to hide from reality (however weak or strong the tendency is). When you judge people problems, take note of how accurate your assessment was. Familiarize yourself with the people or situations you seriously misjudged. With practice, you should be able to improve.

10.3 Summary

In the political process, identifying problems is of critical importance. Because it is dynamic and emotionally taxing, it requires time and energy.

Identifying problems in a disciplined, organized manner helps counterbalance the emotional impact. Use the following guidelines to examine products and people:

☐ For each external deliverable or product needed by the team, look for any obstacles to delivery of a high-quality product on time and within budget.

☐ For each presentation to be made or review to be accepted, look for any reasons for denial of either the approval or a favorable review.

☐ For each player, look for any procedural or protocol omissions, or any disagreement with concept, approach, or content. Also look for negative relationships between yourself and the player or members of his network. Empathize with the player to understand him and his environment better, and be as brutally honest in your assessment of reality as possible. Seeing a problem early allows you to prepare for it and make the best of the situation.

For this activity, use your assessment of the environment, and use your own network to gather all the information available. The result should be a list of useful problem statements, which describe all the existing and potential problems you can see.

Chapter 10: Exercises

1. Review the SCRIMP project as described in Chapters 2 and 5, and compile a list of problem statements from the perspective of Bernie Stone just before his contact with Fred Mandel.

2. Once again, consider your most recent projects. From the perspective of the project manager, make a list of problem statements that depict the situation at critical points in these projects.

3. Now consider your current assignment. From the project manager's perspective, make a list of problem statements that depict the situation as it is now.

11

DEVELOPING SOLUTIONS

During the late summer of 1962, the United States Central Intelligence Agency determined that the Soviet Union was installing defensive missiles in Cuba. The situation was watched with concern; and on October 14, a U-2 reconnaissance flight revealed that launch sites were being built for offensive missiles, with at least one missile already on site and soon to be operational. In addition, it was discovered that Russian ships were en route to Cuba, carrying large numbers of missiles and bombers with nuclear weapons capability. This was the beginning of the Cuban missile crisis.

The action of President John F. Kennedy and his advisors, as described by Arthur M. Schlesinger, Jr., in *A Thousand Days,* represents a brilliant display of political process.* Kennedy believed that installa-

---

*A.M. Schlesinger, Jr., *A Thousand Days: John F. Kennedy in the White House* (Boston: Houghton Mifflin, 1965).

tion by the Russians of offensive weapons ninety miles from the United States was totally unacceptable and would somehow have to be prevented. To deal with the crisis, he assembled an executive committee of his top advisors. Under tight security, Kennedy and the committee spent the next week analyzing the problem and exploring possible solutions.

The committee began by gathering all available intelligence on current Soviet activities, policies, and previous behavior in similar situations. It also considered at great length the personalities, goals, and tendencies of each Soviet leader likely to be involved in the missile installation. Committee members explored a full range of possible reactions — from doing nothing to invading Cuba — examining moves and countermoves, and carefully evaluating the resulting positions. Finally, they decided on a weapons quarantine, to be effected by a blockade of all Soviet shipping into Cuba until the offensive missiles were removed. In a televised speech on Monday, October 22, President Kennedy told the nation of the blockade. The next day, the Organization of American States passed a resolution providing legal basis for the blockade, and Ambassador Adlai Stevenson spoke at the United Nations, telling representatives of the world's countries of the decision.

Kennedy and his committee waited for Soviet reaction. As the ships steamed toward the blockade, the tension mounted. Sensing that the Soviets needed more time, Kennedy moved the blockade closer to Cuba. By Wednesday, October 24, signs appeared indicating that the Soviets were preparing to back off. Kennedy and his advisors believed that any direct military confrontation with the Soviets could escalate to nuclear war, and made sure that an out was provided for a peaceful end to the crisis. Kennedy did this by authorizing Ambassador Stevenson to pursue private discussions with the Soviets on weapons removal. Meanwhile, American troops amassed in southern Florida, preparing to invade Cuba.

Throughout the week, contacts between the two sides were made through ambassadors and various third parties, all searching for a way out of the crisis. By Friday morning, Soviet Premier Nikita Khrushchev had turned his ships around, choosing not to challenge the blockade. But work continued on the missile sites with apparent intent to make the missiles already in Cuba operational.

On Friday afternoon, a Soviet official in Washington suggested some possible terms of agreement to ABC newsman John Scali. Scali quickly passed this information to the White House, stunned that he had been chosen as an intermediary. A few hours later, a cable from

Khrushchev to Kennedy arrived at the White House, confirming that the missiles would be removed in exchange for the end of the quarantine and assurance that the United States would not invade Cuba.

After that apparent easing of the confrontation, Saturday morning brought a second cable, changing the Russian position entirely and demanding that the United States pull out of its Turkish bases in exchange for a Cuban pull-out.

This sent the executive committee into turmoil, but in a committee meeting later that day, Attorney General Robert F. Kennedy proposed that they ignore the second letter and reply to the first. The President seized upon this idea and sent a response indicating his willingness to pursue the first letter, making no mention of the second. At the same time, he passed word through the Soviet ambassador that an invasion would be launched by Tuesday unless assurances were received within twenty-four hours. On Sunday, Khrushchev agreed, and the crisis ended.

Although the stakes in this interaction were unthinkably high, the Schlesinger account describes the rapidly moving events, time pressures, limited information, and apparently unresolvable issues that frequently characterize the political process. The problem was to get the missiles out of Cuba without shifting the balance of power between the United States and the Soviet Union, and without pushing the world into nuclear holocaust. After a careful evaluation, the President and his advisors chose a course of action and made initial moves. They followed Soviet reactions very closely, and decided further actions as the situation developed, making sure that all acceptable avenues were left open. The situation was finally resolved by a brilliant move to disregard what appeared to be a shift back toward confrontation — a creative decision that departed from expected behavior.

It's a good bet that the Soviets were following their variation of the same process, evaluating the players and all the possible moves and countermoves, and then acting and reacting, dynamically repeating the process as events moved on.

There was no one solution. There was a decision on a course of action, and a first set of moves. As the situation developed, more moves were made, each one carefully considered, until finally resolution was reached. And the process did not stop; rather, the crisis took its place as one of many ongoing interactions between the United States and the Soviet Union.

11.1 Formulating a solution

In finding solutions for problems facing your project, you should follow a procedure similar to that described above. Call in any or all of your team members or perhaps members of your network. At least two people, you and one other, should be involved, and preferably three or more. Each person you pick should be trustworthy and insightful.

Start with a clear statement of the problems as you see them. When you have formulated this initial problem statement, assemble all of the information you have that is relevant to the situation. This includes information about the formal organization and relevant procedures, profiles of the players, and any details about their networks. You should also have an accurate statement of the events leading up to the situation.

Everybody involved needs to understand the situation as fully as possible. If they don't, your group could end up making bad decisions based on inaccurate or inadequate data (garbage in, garbage out). Share all of what you know and make sure that everyone agrees about the facts, recognizing that interpretations may still differ.

A period of gestation follows, while the group continues to assimilate the information. This trial-and-error process should produce a final problem statement that fits the available information (although you might decide that a part of the problem is lack of information).

When you are satisfied that you have a good problem statement, explore possible solutions. Look at a full range of alternatives, rather than grabbing at the first idea that appears to be workable. Make a point of having considered several scenarios before making a choice. As a disciplining device, try to have at least three significantly different options.

Each scenario, or course of action, is an approach to solving the problem, and each opens with a series of moves. When put into play, each set of moves is followed by reactions, followed by other actions and further reactions, and so on. In the session, try to anticipate the moves and countermoves as far ahead as possible.

A chess game serves as a good model. Each move you make changes the board position. Your opponent then reacts with his next move, again changing the position for your next move. The successful chess player anticipates the position after each move, his opponent's alternatives and likely moves, and his own resulting alternatives and likely moves, anticipating as far ahead as he can. Using past experiences to recognize good and bad situations and solutions, he picks the best first move. Each time his opponent responds, he repeats the process.

The political chess game has fewer restrictions. The game is not limited to two players, no one need wait his turn, and the capabilities of the players are not fixed as are the moves of chess pieces. Still, each move or change in the situation requires reassessment and possible further response.

The brainstorming group should describe as many rational scenarios as it can, and play out each one until it is seen to fail or to reach a successful solution. When all the options have been explored, pick one. (During the Cuban missile crisis, several scenarios seemed acceptable and a member of the group was appointed advocate for each. Arguments were then heard and debated by the entire group, with the President finally deciding on the quarantine.)

The result of the session is a course of action. This course of action consists of a strategy for solving the problem, the appropriate opening moves, and a general plan for subsequent action. As events unfold, the situation will change. You might even have to discard your plans and go back to the beginning, but if events proceed in anywhere near the direction you anticipated, you're on your way to a solution.

I've described the process for coping with major problems and crises, but it also works for minor problems and annoyances. In fact, if you tend to downplay or overlook minor problems, using the process as described might save you some pain or embarrassment. The seriousness of the situation should determine your reaction and the extent of your planning. However, do not be fooled into judging a situation as minor before you begin your evaluation. Often, only the tip of the iceberg is exposed.

The process for formulating a solution can be summarized as follows:

- ☐ Assemble your problem solving group.
- ☐ Formulate a preliminary problem statement.
- ☐ Collect all relevant information about the situation, the players, and recent events.
- ☐ Assimilate the information and develop a current problem statement.
- ☐ Explore possible scenarios and their probable consequences, until a best course of action emerges.
- ☐ For the chosen course of action, identify the overall strategy, your initial moves, and expected future moves.

11.2 The nature of political solutions

Political solutions involve changing the attitude or actions of someone outside your control. To effect such a change, you must make a fundamental decision: Will the change be accomplished by persuasion or by force? If you can convince someone to change willingly, you probably have preserved or enhanced whatever positive relationship existed between him and you. If you somehow force or manipulate someone into change, you probably have increased the negative aspect of your relationship, or perhaps have created an enemy where one did not previously exist.

Solving problems through force or manipulation has long-term effects. Once you use force or manipulation, it is not soon forgotten; you have made an enemy or at least a non-friend, and future dealings with this person or members of his network (and possibly of their networks) will show the effects of your actions. In plain words, if you decide to play dirty, you'll have to live with it. And since such people will no longer trust you, it will be difficult to return to clean interactions.

Herb Cohen, in *You Can Negotiate Anything,* writes about win/win versus win/lose negotiations.* He points out that, while you can be successful in a win/lose negotiation, it's very difficult to come back for a second transaction with someone you attacked the first time around. If you anticipate an ongoing relationship with someone, it is always in your best interest to look for win/win solutions.

Cohen observes that in most cases you can find win/win solutions by better understanding the other person's true goals and finding ways to satisfy both your goals and his. This may involve looking beyond stated or apparent goals to higher levels (in Chapter 10, my goal of wanting public transportation was, at a higher level, the need for a ride and could be satisfied in other ways).

The issue is more complicated than merely deciding whether to be clean or dirty. The tone or nature of your interactions is at least as important as the interactions themselves, since over time we become known by our actions. Another way to say this is that every action affects your network of relationships as well as the immediate situation. Each time you make contact with one of the players, his image of you and how you interact will enter his mind. If he likes the way you operate, he'll be predisposed to cooperate. He might even feel he owes you one. If he's had unpleasant dealings with you in the past, he's not

---

*H. Cohen, *You Can Negotiate Anything* (New York: Bantam Books, 1982).

likely to be helpful. So, consider the image you project, and how you are perceived by each player. Each move you make should take into account the impact on your image.

11.3 Creative problem solving

A young engineer, employed by the management firm of a large high-rise office building, was called to his boss's office. The boss said he had received many complaints about the elevators being too slow, and told the engineer to do what he could to solve the problem.

A week later the engineer returned to announce he had a solution. Pleased, the boss sat back to listen, expecting to hear about increased elevator speeds, a new algorithm for servicing the floors, and so on. Instead, the engineer proposed the installation of mirrors on each floor next to the elevator. If people were kept busy checking their appearance, he explained, they would be less likely to notice the wait.

While the boss had seen the problem as one of speeding up the elevator service, the engineer looked at it differently. He chose to attack the impatience of the people waiting rather than the speed of the elevators. This little story illustrates the traps we build for ourselves in looking for solutions. We make assumptions that aren't required but somehow seem to be, and we limit our solutions to ideas that we derived logically from our assumptions.

An old but classic example of this trap is illustrated in Fig. 11.1. The problem is to connect the nine dots by making four straight lines without lifting the pencil from the page. The dots seem to form a boundary that cannot be violated, but the lines do not have to remain within the boundary. The solution, shown in Fig. 11.2, can only be found by breaking this barrier and extending the lines outside the area defined by the dots.

Figure 11.1. Connect-the-dots problem.

In the project environment, the political barriers are formed by the culture, or system of interactions, that has grown up around the project and its players. From that culture come the implicit rules or traditions that are followed not only without question, but without thought. These implicit rules are guides to expected behavior. They smoothe the flow of activity, but also act as constraints. They constrain not by imposing laws, but simply by example and precedent. And by constraining behavior, they also constrain ideas about what behavior is possible.

Change, by Watzlawick et al., addresses this dilemma in the context of family systems.* While project players form a somewhat different environment, the same principles apply. The authors identify at least two levels of change: change that is within the rules of the system, and change that breaks or alters these rules of behavior. By changing only within the rules, the system is perpetuated, but change that breaks the rules creates a new system with new boundaries.

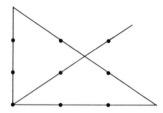

Figure 11.2. Connect-the-dots solution.

During the Cuban missile crisis, when the second Khrushchev cable arrived apparently nullifying the first, the natural inclination was to react to the new Soviet position. Robert Kennedy's suggestion to act as if the second letter never arrived broke the rules of interaction. It allowed the Soviets to reconsider a potentially disastrous move and required that they resubmit it if they really meant it.

Solutions usually can be found within the expected system, but there are times when it is valuable or necessary to break through the barriers in search of a solution. Creative solutions break these barriers; without them, sooner or later you'll be stuck.

The ability to conceive of creative, rule-breaking ideas is a talent some of us possess more than others. Using a group to solve problems opens the door to more creative solutions by increasing the likelihood that someone will have a good idea, particularly if the group encourages different ideas. So, keep an eye out for creative people, and use them liberally in political problem solving.

---

*P. Watzlawick, J.H. Weakland, and R. Fisch, *Change: Principles of Problem Formation and Problem Resolution* (New York: W.W. Norton, 1974).

To a certain extent, creative problem solving can be learned. Edward de Bono, in *Lateral Thinking,* provides a set of techniques for overcoming the mental constructs that inhibit new approaches.* Lateral thinking provides ways to challenge and temporarily suspend these constructs, allowing new ideas to take their place.

11.4 Political moves

No discussion of political solutions would be complete without some descriptions of the moves or techniques that are often used. Moves are the lowest level of activity, the mechanism by which the strategies and courses of action are carried out.

As a matter of self-preservation, you should have some familiarity with political moves, especially the dirty ones. Your ability to see a move coming might allow you to duck or counter. The following list briefly describes some of the general categories of moves. As with most of my lists, I make no claim to completeness, so add to it and adjust it to fit your own observations.

☐ *Entrapment:* deliberately creating a situation to let a person's tendencies get him in trouble. If your opponent has a temper, you put him into a situation in which he will lose it unwisely. If he is easily tempted, you tempt him with something he shouldn't take. When the bait is taken, the trap closes and the victim is caught. Blackmail sometimes follows, since getting caught may mean there is now a secret. Not very nice? You bet.

☐ *Direct frontal assault:* use of threats, intimidation, or actual invocation of one's authority or physical power to force the opponent to back off or fail

☐ *Invoking higher authority:* convincing someone in a position of higher authority to rule either in your favor or against your opponent. Direct presentations, meetings, or lobbying with those in positions of authority are typical ways of invoking authority. Less common approaches in business are legal actions and publicity. One of many variations is to make a deal with someone who has the authority you need, in exchange for the authority you have.

☐ *False statements:* another big category that includes euphemisms, double talk, lies, and even bold statements that black is white. If

---

*E. de Bono, *Lateral Thinking: Creativity, Step by Step* (New York: Harper & Row, 1970).

you deny the obvious loudly enough, it may stop some people for at least a while. Governments are good at this: Since the public attention span is relatively short, false statements can defuse the pressure long enough for the public and the press to lose interest.

☐ *Smear tactics:* use of facts, distortions, or outright lies to attack and discredit a person or group. As with false statements, smears are often used as diversionary moves to avoid blame or attention.

☐ *Expert witness:* use of an acknowledged (or apparent) expert, such as a consultant or noted authority, to sway opinions

☐ *Bluff:* includes two types: Make your opponents believe you have what you don't, and make them believe you don't have what you do. As good poker players will tell you, when they don't think you have it, they throw more into the pot. The bluff causes the other side to back off, look elsewhere, or come at you when it shouldn't.

☐ *Inaction:* includes both stalling and doing nothing, although they really are different. A stall is trying to buy time until something else happens (the cavalry arrives or the pressure eases), whereas doing nothing presumes that maintaining the status quo is the best strategy.

☐ *Deadline pressure:* invoking a deadline to force someone into action (or inaction) he otherwise might not take. Moves might be constructed around a real deadline, or an artificial deadline can be created. An ultimatum is an obvious type of deadline. More subtle deadlines appear to be accidental (for example, a proposal presented in late December that must be acted upon by the end of the year). It is no coincidence that most labor disputes are resolved just before a strike deadline.

☐ *Appeasement:* taking the underdog position. In the animal world, the term is submission. This is often thought of as cowardice, but it might be strategy instead. Underdogs get their way more often than you think, and appear deceptively harmless.

☐ *Ignoring orders:* continuing as if nothing happened. This can be a countermove to invoking higher authority.

☐ *Hanging tough:* good old-fashioned tenacity — give only what you have and keep chipping away at the opposition's resistance

☐ *Issue confrontation:* discussion and confrontation of issues (not of personalities) in an attempt to reach a mutually agreeable solution. This may lead to negotiation or arbitration.

Most of these entries tend to fall on the dirty pool side of the ledger. There seem to be a lot more ways to be devious than to be straight. The only category that is always clean is issue confrontation. Use of expert witnesses, hanging tough, appeasement, and inaction can also be decent moves. The other actions take on varying degrees of nastiness depending on the actual move and the circumstances.

For example, let's look back at Smoot and the actions that saved the SCRIMP project. Bernie Stone's first instinct was to confront issues. He presented the issues to Ralph Johnson, whose response was to claim LM&C's expertise, but whose actual move was inaction (his real reason was lack of concern, and belief that Hardmyer and Woods would not go against the LM&C report — an envisioned higher authority). Stone then invoked his own higher authority in the person of Fred Mandel.

Mandel in turn lobbied with his fellow SMC members, possibly making some deals, and invoked the expert testimony of Steve Silva (representing the Materials organization) at the special SMC meeting to discredit the LM&C report and start the new study. He also flexed his own authority by funding the study and thereby taking control of it.

Finally, Barnwell fired Woods to discredit him and point the finger away from himself, an exercise in using direct authority to carry out a smear tactic and appease the organization's need to assign blame.

11.5 Staying in control

While the moves are fascinating to observe and are generally the most colorful part of the political process, far more important issues are keeping track of events, and acting from a plan or strategy rather than reacting to circumstance. Good solutions come from anticipating problems and planning long-term strategies that pursue goals in a well-thought-out manner.

Events, organizational structures, and sometimes people conspire to generate political problems. Since problems will continue to arise, sometimes with more frequency than anyone would like, the game is not one move or one problem or even one project. The game will continue as long as the players are there. And as long as you are there, you'll probably have to work with them. If you play the game clean instead of dirty, you'll sleep better at night, be able to look yourself in the mirror in the morning, and won't get a stiff neck from looking back over your shoulder during the day.

Chapter 11: Exercises

1. Again, look at the Smoot example. What overall course of action d
    Stone and Mandel adopt? What other courses of action could the
    have considered?

2. Match the moves in the account of the Cuban missile crisis to th
    categories in this chapter.

3. How do you develop solutions to political problems? How does you
    approach differ from this one? Is it more or less effective? Why?

12

SCRIMP REVISITED

12.1 Smoot: Act III

Although Bernie Stone had received no formal training in the politics of projects, he seemed to gravitate to an organized political process. During the SCRIMP Requirements Study, for instance, he found it useful to spend about two hours a week reviewing the effort. Each Wednesday at 3:00 p.m., he and his team reviewed technical issues and then assessed the external political situation for potential problems. This weekly session kept Bernie and the team alert and confident that they could handle whatever problems arose.

The study had taken a total of four months, which included time to get SMC approval to develop the new SCRIMP. During that period, the various managers in the Materials organization were favorably impressed with SCRIMP. The organization, from Mandel on down, anticipated that the system would provide badly needed inventory control.

Although the study had been quite successful, inventory costs at Smoot were rapidly increasing and the recession was taking its toll on revenues. The existing system was unable to control inventory levels, and Mandel was under significant pressure to reduce costs. Barnwell, still smarting from the rejected LM&C report, got to Mandel's boss, Chuck McLear. He pointed out that the new SCRIMP had taken four months for a second study and, since it would not use the LM&C software package, would add another eight months to the original schedule, putting it a full year behind the proposed LM&C timetable.

McLear, already pressured by inventory problems, was not about to let Barnwell hold that one against him. He told Mandel (who now was officially responsible for SCRIMP) that the original sixteen-month schedule must be met, that the clock had started four months ago, and that the damn thing had better bring the inventory costs under control.

During the SCRIMP study, Bernie had grown fairly secure in his relationship with Mandel. They had talked frequently, and he had learned much from Mandel about the political world at Smoot. When Mandel told him of the sixteen-month deadline, Bernie felt free to balk. He said that he could not meet the date, that the original LM&C system could not have met it either, and that the deadline came from a bad estimate and was absurd. Bernie was stunned at the violence with which Mandel's fist hit the desk as he shouted, "That's the way it has to be!"

To make matters worse, resources were still limited. Of the six people on the study team, only Bernie, Marsha, and Jack had computing skills; the other team members were functioning as user analysts. Moreover, only five additional people would be available from Information Systems, including the two maintenance programmers on the existing inventory system. That gave Bernie ten people one year to do a job currently estimated at twenty-nine person-years.

The pressure was slightly alleviated when Bernie was able to confirm that the Operations Planning group within Information Systems would be responsible for all hardware acquisition and installation, and that Larry Casey's Database Administration group would take on the database design. In addition, following completion of detailed user requirements, Steve Silva would move back to Materials to head up the effort to prepare the user community for SCRIMP. Silva would be responsible for user training, writing new procedures, acceptance testing, and preparing all the information that would be passed on to the users.

During the study, team members had been exposed to structured analysis, and Bernie planned to use the structured techniques throughout the project. He hoped that the use of these techniques would result in at least a thirty percent improvement in productivity. He estimated that the improved productivity, in combination with the off-loaded database and user-related tasks, would reduce his manpower needs to about nineteen person-years. With these plans, SCRIMP would only be one year late — still terrible, but a lot better than two years late.

The Wednesday afternoon meeting that followed Bernie's encounter with Mandel was devoted to the resource problem. Although Mandel didn't say why McLear was so inflexible about the timetable, his reference to the LM&C schedule was enough to indicate Barnwell's influence. If Barnwell was involved, the team probably could expect little support from IS. In fact, Bernie thought it not out of the question that IS management, pressured from the top by Barnwell, would make it difficult for SCRIMP to succeed. It was a possible explanation for the meager resources he had been given.

Bernie also guessed that his immediate manager, Ralph Johnson, blamed him for the ouster of the LM&C report. Since the study began, Johnson had become less and less supportive of his efforts. And considering that Hardmyer was the acting vice-president of IS, Bernie was surprised that he was getting any cooperation from Database Administration or Operations Planning.

So, the SCRIMP team ruled out additional IS resources as a solution to the dilemma. With the deadline fixed, Bernie saw two alternatives: Hire contract programmers to carry part of the load, or reduce the project's scope. The team members agreed that if IS management was resisting SCRIMP, they would not be willing to hire contract help, so Mandel would have to fund it. That would require a significant change in Smoot policy, and Bernie sensed that Mandel was in no mood to welcome any further expense. As to reduced scope, after shooting down LM&C and proposing their alternative to the SMC, Bernie would be unwise to suddenly announce that the new SCRIMP was really more than Smoot needed.

Marsha hit on a solution: McLear wanted the deadline met, but what he really wanted, she thought, was a system that could begin reducing his inventory levels in twelve months. So why not partition the system? If they could implement enough function by the deadline to begin reducing inventory, with the remaining functions developed later, McLear might be satisfied.

In fact, they were able to split the system and provide in the first piece what they thought was enough function to help reduce the inventory. On Friday, they handed the proposal to Mandel. He accepted the idea and conveyed it to McLear, who also approved. Both were relieved that Bernie had found a way to meet the deadline, and were confident that this was enough to defuse Barnwell. They decided that Bernie would present the schedule for the two-phase cutover (the first phase of which would meet the twelve-month deadline) at the next SMC meeting. McLear would attend and lend his support, and again Mandel would do the lobbying (although most of the other SMC members were relatively uninvolved).

With these plans barely finalized, Bernie received two memos that knocked him off his feet. The first, from Larry Casey, indicated that the database help might cost him much more than it would give him. To do a proper job of database design, Casey indicated, his group must model data requirements for the entire Materials and Manufacturing operations, with some possible analysis of engineering and financial requirements as well. Casey proposed a schedule that was significantly beyond the SCRIMP timetable.

The second memo was from Evan Smith, manager of Technical Support, informing Bernie that SCRIMP's plan to use the structured techniques was not compatible with the FORMS methodology and would not be allowed. Not only did this news kill Bernie's hoped-for thirty percent productivity gain, but FORMS, and its mountains of paperwork, probably would cause a productivity *loss*. No one had yet used FORMS, but it came with a $90 thousand price tag — and Smith was committed to its use.

Totally frustrated, the entire SCRIMP team headed for the local pub. As the pitchers kept coming, they blew off steam about the ridiculous environment in which they worked. It was well after midnight when the last of the group staggered home.

They had needed a good gripe session. But even though he had been able to let loose his own frustration, Bernie could not shake the problems. He was concerned about the immediate situation and was disturbed by the increasingly apparent resistance from his own organization. He was angry, and felt an intense dislike for Barnwell, Hardmyer, Johnson, and now Smith and Casey. How could anybody get a job done with their roadblocks?

On Monday, Bernie's mood was sober and determined. With Marsha and Steve, he began analysis of their new dilemma. Time needed to be spent to prepare the SMC phasing proposal for the following week, but the new problems needed to be dealt with first.

After some discussion, they isolated two problem areas:

1. They recognized the value of data requirements modeling and wanted the expertise of the database group. The team also needed the extra people. The problem was to use this expertise and somehow limit the scope to fit SCRIMP and its timetable.

2.   To meet the twelve-month deadline for the first phase
      of SCRIMP, the team needed the productivity im-
      provements of the structured techniques, and it also
      needed to avoid the overhead required by the FORMS
      methodology.

They recognized that Larry Casey was dedicated to the data
modeling approach to system development. Although competent,
Casey was almost impossible to sway in his opinions, especially about
anything related to database. Since he reported through Evan Smith up
to Hardmyer and Barnwell, any direct appeal to higher management
would probably fall on deaf ears. But they doubted that Casey was part
of a move toward political resistance. He was a technician, and probably unaware of any political interactions surrounding SCRIMP.

The solution seemed to come down either to using Casey's people
on his terms or to proceeding without his support. The team members
agreed that they might be able to influence the data modelers once they
had been assigned to SCRIMP, but that Casey probably would keep
tabs on their progress and ultimately would control their scope.

Almost ready to throw in the towel and not use Casey's support,
Bernie had an idea: The higher authority that was strong enough to
redirect Casey was the SMC. If team members could get an SMC rul-
ing to redirect data modeling to SCRIMP's requirements, they would
get what they needed.

He decided to approach Casey by resisting his proposed scope.
After Casey's predictable argument, Bernie would first refuse his help
and then offer him a deal. He would invite Casey to present his approach at the next SMC session. If the SMC accepted, Bernie would go
along. If not, they would reduce the scope to SCRIMP only. He felt
that Casey would not want to miss the opportunity to build the database
for SCRIMP, and would be hooked by the prospect of attending an
SMC meeting.

He planned not to tell Larry Casey of the imposed twelve-month
deadline, hoping that Larry's lack of experience would cause him to
make a poor showing at the SMC. If Larry looked bad enough, Hardmyer and Barnwell could not support him, and Bernie would get what
he wanted. The problem was to get Casey in front of the SMC without
advance warning to his bosses. It was a bit risky and not very nice, but
Bernie thought they could pull it off. True, Larry Casey would end up
with some mud on his face, but the frustrations caused by the IS resistance and limitations had made the team more than willing to consider
such unpleasant approaches.

The FORMS issue was another matter. Team members agreed
that discussions with Evan Smith would be fruitless, since Smith had

recommended the initial purchase of FORMS and could not see its inadequacies. Approaching the SMC with this issue would invite an open debate on an established policy with a $90 thousand investment — they were unlikely to win.

Marsha suggested to the group that they review FORMS and propose a modified version, incorporating the structured techniques. After some discussion, they concluded that FORMS had so much red tape that a reasonable modification would be too radical for Smith to accept, especially for its first use.

Then Silva proposed that they ignore Smith and do it their own way. They should respond verbally to Smith that they intended to use FORMS. When Smith discovered that they were not, they would simply tell him that, since they started requirements definition during the study using structured analysis, they planned to adopt FORMS when the requirements specification was complete. When requirements were completed, they could then announce that, based on their commitment to structured analysis, it made more sense to continue using the structured techniques on SCRIMP, and to begin using FORMS on another project that could adopt it from the beginning. The longer they resisted FORMS, the less sense it would make to use it.

While this approach would not increase Bernie's popularity within IS, he was already at odds with his management and didn't think it would make the relationship any worse. (It probably would, but the truth was that Bernie didn't care. If things did not improve, he planned to leave after SCRIMP.) The group adjourned, somewhat tainted by their schemes, but convinced that they had chosen solutions that would work.

The database ploy worked. Larry Casey's presentation was a last-minute change to the SMC agenda. At 4:45 p.m. on the day before the meeting, Mandel called Hardmyer. Mandel let him know that Bernie and Casey had agreed to present the issue of data modeling to the SMC. Hardmyer balked, but it was too late to change, since the revised agenda was already being distributed along with copies of Casey's presentation.

The next morning, Casey addressed the SMC in a language that none of them understood: database. The presentation was confusing and technical, and when they saw his timetable for the SCRIMP-related data modeling, Smith, Hardmyer, and Barnwell groaned quietly. The approach was rejected.

When Bernie followed with his phased-cutover presentation, he suggested that the data modeling might fit nicely if they limited scope to SCRIMP only, since it would not delay the cutovers. The SMC members, in technical confusion, grunted approval. After the meeting,

Casey thanked Bernie for coming to his rescue. Bernie shuddered and barely managed a smile.

With the phased approach also accepted, development proceeded. Larry Casey continued as database manager, but after two months was stripped of his title in an "economic cutback." He did not understand that his abortive SMC presentation was the cause, but once he got over the demotion, he was actually relieved to be able to concentrate more freely on technical matters.

Evan Smith discovered that SCRIMP was not using FORMS when the requirements specification was published some three months after the SMC session. The fait accompli of the specification and the rational argument that FORMS should begin on a project not yet started left Smith with very few reactions other than his own frustration.

Although the immediate obstacles were pushed aside, SCRIMP was not yet out of the woods. Still to come were problems with test-time availability, terminal selection from a vendor about to go out of business, strange reactions to their specifications from auditors who had never seen a specification using structured techniques, and continued resistance from Bernie's management. But it is appropriate to leave the SCRIMP odyssey and recap what has happened.

12.2 Analysis

The SCRIMP team's goals continue to be closely aligned with its user, Materials. In spite of the roadblocks, the goal of a useful, effective system has not been compromised. In fact, it is this very alignment of goals with the user that has caused Bernie Stone's alienation from his own management. In this situation, it has not been possible to maintain goal alignment with both the user and with IS. Also, a bit of vengeance has crept into Bernie's motivations, not enough perhaps to divert him and his group from building the system, but enough for them to use some unpleasant means to get their way.

Bernie, Steve, and Marsha exhibit an ability to assess the environment. They understand the inventory squeeze that is motivating Mandel and McLear, and clearly see Barnwell's influence. Smith's commitment to FORMS is understood, as is Casey's tunnel vision. And the SCRIMP team's appreciation of the IS resistance is significant. To understand that your own management is actually undermining your assignment takes some willingness to perceive unpleasant reality.

The SCRIMP weekly problem sessions are very successful. Bernie has devised an effective means to spot problems before they get totally out of hand. In those sessions, the team members demonstrate ability to prepare valid problem statements, which show a sound appreciation of the issues. They identify three discrete problems: the lack of resources needed to meet the sixteen-month deadline, the conflict between use of the methodology and the structured techniques, and the data modeling scope issue.

One problem they missed was the subcontracting of hardware selection to the Operations Planning group (which would select remote hardware that was functionally inept and that was from a vendor on the verge of bankruptcy). This issue, as with the methodology and data modeling issues, is rooted in Smoot's organizational fragmentation, which does not give Bernie full control, but forces him to accept policies and decisions that may compromise his project.

The SCRIMP team's group process allowed it to explore many solutions to each problem. Team members brought to bear their knowledge of the players' motivations and networks, and were able to explore each scenario a few moves down the line. For political process, they get high marks.

12.3 Moves

It is also useful to examine the political moves that took place. Barnwell set up the resource and deadline problems with a direct threat to McLear. The message was, If you don't bring SCRIMP up in sixteen months, I'm going to announce your poor decision to higher authorities. Due to the inventory cost pressure, McLear would have put pressure on SCRIMP anyway; but without Barnwell's veiled threats, the deadline probably would not have been so arbitrary or firm.

McLear responded by appeasing Barnwell and dropping the ball in Mandel's lap; Mandel did the same to Bernie. This was the first evidence of Mandel's temperament when cornered, and Bernie quickly absorbed it. He decided against asking for contract programmers, in part because of Mandel's mood.

Bernie, caught between a rock and a hard place, did not become horrible to live with. Instead, with the help of his teammates, he looked for a realistic solution. The solution was creative, relying on their perception of Barnwell's involvement and McLear and Mandel's real needs. They also used the twelve-month deadline to get acceptance of less than a full system. (A partial implementation may have been acceptable for other reasons, but their position was, the deadline is impossible, so here is a compromise that will help inventory and get you off Barnwell's hook.) They also used the authority of the SMC to get approval of the two-phased approach, avoiding potential resistance from IS later in the project.

With the database dilemma, Bernie's behavior was not as pure. Casey used his authority as database manager to insist on a much broader modeling scope than was needed by SCRIMP. Rather than cooperate, he used muscle. The SCRIMP team understood his bull-headedness and his lack of political acumen, and played a fairly subtle game of entrapment. First, Bernie jousted with Casey, and threatened not to use him at all. Then, knowing that Casey was not an effective communicator, he enticed him to speak at the SMC. To do this, he needed Mandel's cooperation in informing Hardmyer before the meeting, but after it was too late to change the agenda or the presentation (a form of deadline pressure). Finally, Bernie played expert to the SMC, suggesting that the database approach would work if the scope were reduced. Casey, with total lack of insight, actually thanked Bernie and left with no understanding of the setup or the consequences to him.

For those of you who cringed at Bernie's unscrupulous maneuver, I hasten to point out that, if Casey had not tried to intimidate the project team, he would not have lost his position. Entrapment uses the tendencies of the individual to get himself in trouble. The mouse would not get caught if he didn't like cheese.

The FORMS battle, while also not nice, had no consequences for Evan Smith. Rather, any project *using* FORMS would suffer, since FORMS was not well conceived, and Smith had elected to enforce it verbatim. The $90 thousand price tag had blinded him and others (including the SMC, which had approved the purchase a year earlier).

Smith exercised his authority to enforce FORMS. Significantly, he wrote a memo instead of dropping by Bernie's office or telephoning to discuss the matter. This was not a friendly gesture, but a power move. He was aware of the IS vendetta against SCRIMP, and felt secure in attacking; he also wanted to show his bosses that he was aligned against SCRIMP (a form of appeasement).

The SCRIMP team members responded with a lie, deliberately implying they would use FORMS but having no intention of doing so. The lie was to serve as a diversion until requirements were complete. At that point, they could innocently point out that in spite of their good intentions, it no longer made sense to change over from structured techniques (deadline pressure).

12.4 SCRIMP's status

SCRIMP seems to be in good shape. As I pointed out, there are more obstacles ahead, but the group is well equipped to deal with them. Its goal is to build a good system, useful to the users, and its political process is well oiled. The group is determined and responds well under pressure (better in fact than everyone around them).

The SCRIMP team has, however, contributed to its own poor position in the IS organization. Virtually every political move has alienated it from IS management. While you could argue that IS started it by ignoring the problems with the LM&C report, Bernie and his team moved against IS rather than finding a solution with them — and now each new move on either side increases the gulf between them. (This is not to excuse IS management, which somehow has let personal agendas prevent it from supporting a project that is vital to the financial health of Smoot.)

The situation is not too likely to hurt Steve Silva; he works in another organization; and since Marsha's political contributions are not visible outside the team, there may be no repercussions to her beyond being branded a member of SCRIMP. It is Bernie Stone who is politically affected. He likely will never have a decent relationship with Barnwell, Hardmyer, Johnson, or Evan Smith, and perhaps members of their networks. Since they are the current political power in Bernie's organization, they will probably depose him as soon as he slips up or is beyond Mandel's influence. Bernie will need to look over his shoulder for trouble for quite a while.

On the other hand, he may have a patron in Fred Mandel. They clearly work well together, and Mandel no doubt appreciates Bernie's efforts to keep SCRIMP on track. More important, they like and respect each other. If Bernie chooses to stay, he might be able to move to the Materials organization. Or, if Mandel rises within Smoot, he could bring Bernie along. In fact, Bernie's political sense and his coolness under fire might someday take him past Mandel in the organization.

Chapter 12: Exercises

1. Examine the three problems solved by the SCRIMP team, and outline other effective solutions.

2. Given the situation that exists between Bernie Stone and his own management, can you identify any strategy for Bernie that would ease the pressure and move toward positive, or at least kid-gloves, relationships? What would be your first move? Play out the scenario.

3. If you were in Hardmyer's position, how would you view Stone and Mandel's political interactions?

13

THE ONGOING POLITICAL PROCESS

Political problems don't wait politely in the wings until the current act is over. With the heavy and often chaotic load of activities that typifies a project, it's difficult to spot problems before they become crises and demand total attention. In Chapters 6 through 11, I presented a process for dealing with political problems, but it's easy to see how any semblance of process can be lost in the thrashing about that can occur while dealing with daily events.

My own sensing filters aren't always tuned to the right events. Since I can't rely on my interrupt mechanisms to warn me of danger, the way I have been most successful at coping with the environment is to discipline myself in the use of the process. I suggest this discipline not only as a way to begin using the process, but also as an ongoing approach.

13.1 The weekly sessions

Pick a time during the week when you are least likely to be interrupted. Schedule one to three hours. Be absolute in your resolve to use this time every week for attending to political process. Select a team, consisting of the people you want to include in political problem solving. Obviously, they should be trusted, insightful, and creative. They should also have some involvement in the project and a vested interest similar to your own.

During the first session, work on goals (Chapter 7). Examine the goals of the project, and decide which are most critical. Probe your own personal goals and those of your teammates. If personal goals conflict with project goals, your first priority should be to resolve the conflicts. Next, take an inventory of your political skills and capabilities using the table in Chapter 8. Do the same for your teammates. If you have trouble exploring your personal goals and capabilities in a group, do it alone. But also realize that you might have less insight without help.

Next, document your network and those of the other team members. If some relationships aren't as strong or as current as you would like them to be, make some appropriate contact.

At the next session, work on the environment (Chapter 9). First, assemble a model of the formal organization and procedures. Then, build profiles for the frequently contacted players, especially those with whom you will be working immediately. Next, identify significant network relationships among the players, probably by building an influence diagram.

Your assessment of goals and capabilities will probably be stable. Briefly review them every two to three months. If you think they have changed, adjust your evaluations. The environment will be more volatile than goals and capabilities. Each week, as part of your session, add profiles and network data until all the players have been addressed. Review the profiles you have already developed, adjusting them as you acquire new information. If you lack information, make a conscious effort to get what you need, using your network and those of your political teammates.

The remainder of each session should be devoted to problem identification (Chapter 10). Before developing solutions, consider each player, each product, and any outside events that might generate problems. Then, formulate preliminary problem statements for all the problems you see. Now derive solutions to the problems following the process presented in Chapter 11.

If your project is going poorly, you might be too busy to notice new problems. If it is progressing well, you may be lulled into a false sense of security and confidence. In either case, discipline is essential. Run these review sessions every week (more frequently if necessary), and be alert for any change that could lead to new problems.

If you're new to this game or not very good at it, weekly sessions and formal lists, charts, and profiles will help you to improve. As you learn, adapt the process to fit your abilities and personality, but recognize that there must be a process. As soon as the discipline of following a process stops, you become vulnerable to unforeseen events.

Now, as a last exercise, address a current political problem and try to resolve it using the processes described in Chapters 6 through 11. I suggest you try the exercise at the office with one or two other involved people.

13.2 Final comments

I have presented the political process as an organized, disciplined series of steps. If you follow it, you should increase your ability to function and survive in the political arena of projects. Using the process itself as a foundation, I present some comments on the remaining pages about other issues that can be significant to your political survival and growth.

13.2.1 The successful politician

There are six characteristics shared by virtually all successful politicians. These characteristics constitute the essence of politics and are supported and encouraged by the process. If you have developed these characteristics, and if you use them in a disciplined manner, it is likely that you are politically very capable.

The first two characteristics are introspection and control. A good politician is able to understand his own goals and motivations. He can see what drives him as well as which behaviors and motivations harm him. With this awareness, he controls his emotional reactions and directs himself toward his goals. His awareness and control make him less susceptible to the ploys and tricks of his political opposition, and much more efficient in pursuit of his own goals.

The third characteristic is insight into the goals and motivations of others. A good politician is able to read the players in his arena, and to understand what they want and need. This insight allows him to devise solutions that work, since workable solutions inevitably involve changing the opinions or actions of the players.

Accurate perception of reality is fourth. Many of us are plagued by wishful thinking, or by suspicions that things are going wrong when they actually are under control. The successful politician objectively sees what is happening, whether it is good, bad, or indifferent. With this objective assessment, he is able to identify problems accurately, and then monitor the effectiveness of his solutions.

The next characteristic is the ability to think creatively and to recognize and accept creative ideas from others. Without the vision to break and remake the rules, sooner or later a problem will arise that defies solution.

Finally, there is tenacity. The good politician persists when his goals are at stake. He is willing to continue when the situation appears bleak, and to suffer through the tough times. When his opponent wearies and goes home, he is the victor. Tenacity is the most significant quality characterizing a winning politician.

13.2.2 Long-term effects

More important than immediate victory or defeat in the political arena is your reputation among the current and future players. Each of us has a political personality, expressed in the way we react to situations and in the moves we make. This personality often changes as we grow and learn. The players have their own image of this personality, each slightly different, and none likely to be current. Rather, those images are a product of our past interactions, and particularly of those interactions that significantly impressed each player.

Once the image of your personality is established in another player's mind, it is difficult to change it. To undo a positive image, direct evidence is needed, each sample chipping away at the image. To make a negative image positive, large amounts of evidence are needed that show no indication of previous negative moves.

13.2.3 Playing hardball

Political interaction is often competitive. When ideologies or career goals are at stake, and occasionally when little is at stake, some people play rough. These people choose to play the game as a win/lose battle, and dirty moves and tenacious persistence characterize their actions.

Some of them succeed, if attaining power is the measure of success, and some of the top spots in organizational hierarchies are occupied by brutal, win/lose politicians. They live in a world of manipulation and deceit, where no one is trusted and few, if any, are valued.

If you are just beginning your political career, look out. A political neophyte can be brushed aside by a hardball player before he knows what hit him. The project arena is generally safe for learning and establishing your political personality, but if you should happen upon a hardball player, do your best to avoid him. Unless you have had some experience and have seen the rough stuff, you will probably lose and lose badly. If you have to ask yourself if you're ready for hardball, the answer is no.

13.2.4 Ethics and morality

With the exception of a few comments, I have avoided passing judgment on the ethics and morality of hardball politics or of any other sort of politics. However, I do have some opinions, which I present as a last topic in this book.

First, I believe that the political process is neutral to ethics and morality. The ability to be good or evil, and to conduct yourself in a trustworthy or dastardly manner, is not dictated by politics or the political process. Rather, it is a personal choice.

However, I would be remiss to deny any connection. Exposure to the political process does increase the possibility of being politically abusive. For example, in the first Smoot chapter, Bernie Stone is a politically naive, apparently moral, decent person. As events transpire, he uses some rather nasty, premeditated moves to get his way. You could argue that the other players were also nasty; but for whatever reason, Bernie made the choice to play dirty. His actions led to the firing of one person (Woods), the demotion of another (Casey), and the discrediting of a consulting firm (LM&C). He also contributed to an ever-widening gap between his team and his organization, all for the sake of SCRIMP.

The point is that exposure to the political environment and the political process leaves you with a dilemma of how to conduct yourself. If you are politically active, in time it is certain that people will do very nasty things to you. So, the opportunity and the temptation to play dirty will be there, first as a means of fighting back and then perhaps as a way of being.

It is, of course, your choice. But I encourage you to consider the very significant issue of human decency in all your political actions, not because it will help you get your way, but because it is ultimately necessary for survival and simply the way to be.

Epilogue

While the SCRIMP team continued its struggle toward implementation, things were changing in Information Systems. The pressure was rumored to come from very high, but wherever it came from, the first sign of change was announcement of a transfer of duties between Hardmyer and Matt Fitzmorris, director of Operations. It was a lateral swap, moving Hardmyer to Operations director and Fitzmorris to director of Systems and Programming, but with Fitzmorris also becoming acting vice-president.

The second bombshell followed in three months: A high-level reorganization moved IS out from under Barnwell. Barnwell would keep his other responsibilities, and Fitzmorris, who was then confirmed as the new vice-president of Information Systems, would report directly to Group Vice-President Bob Kappler.

McLear was behind the reorganization. Barnwell had played his hand pretty hard, and McLear did not like Barnwell's handling of the Information Systems organization. He convinced Kappler and President Al Straus that a change was in order. The position of director of Systems and Programming, vacated by Fitzmorris, was given to Bill Straus. Bill was the other manager of Systems and Programming along with Ralph Johnson, and also happened to be Al Straus's nephew.

So, by the time SCRIMP faced its initial cutover, the chain of command had been altered drastically, with Straus and Fitzmorris above Johnson, who once again was thinking of early retirement.

The cutover itself went well. Bernie had managed to cope nicely with the additional problems he faced, the most critical of which was getting the terminal hardware selection switched to a more reliable vendor. He survived, and was now a veteran. He had developed a reputation as being tough-minded and goal-oriented, as well as being someone who did not like to compromise or back off.

While he and Bill Straus were not particularly close, they respected each other, and Straus believed that Bernie was the kind of person IS needed to get the job done. One month after the cutover, Bernie was promoted to manager of Systems and Programming, taking over Johnson's area, including SCRIMP, while Johnson moved to cover the slot originally vacated by Straus. Marsha was promoted to SCRIMP project manager and would carry it through the remaining cutover.

A remarkable series of events had turned Bernie Stone's career around — from outhouse to penthouse! The betting was that Straus would make rapid progress through the organization, based on his family ties and his competence, and that Bernie would follow at least to the level of director. Johnson knew he would be out if that happened, and thought even harder about early retirement.

SCRIMP was to become the most successful system yet developed at Smoot, and Bernie Stone became someone you did not want to cross politically. He could see that his next move was up to director, and waited patiently for Straus to be promoted or for Hardmyer to move out.

Bibliography

Berne, E. *Games People Play.* New York: Grove Press, 1964.

_____. *What Do You Say After You Say Hello?* New York: Grove Press, 1972.

Brooks, F.P., Jr. *The Mythical Man-Month.* Reading, Mass.: Addison-Wesley, 1975.

Cohen, H. *You Can Negotiate Anything.* New York: Bantam Books, 1982.

De Bono, E. *Lateral Thinking: Creativity, Step by Step.* New York: Harper & Row, 1970.

DeMarco, T. *Controlling Software Projects: Management, Measurement & Estimation.* New York: Yourdon Press, 1982.

Dickinson, B. *Developing Structured Systems: A Methodology Using Structured Techniques.* New York: Yourdon Press, 1981.

Gildersleeve, T.R. *Data Processing Project Management.* New York: Van Nostrand Reinhold, 1974.

Kepner, C.H., and B.B. Tregoe. *The Rational Manager.* Princeton, N.J.: Kepner-Tregoe, Inc., 1965.

Rogers, C.R. *On Becoming a Person.* Boston: Houghton Mifflin, 1961.

Thomsett, R. *People & Project Management.* New York: Yourdon Press, 1980.

Townsend, R. *Up the Organization.* New York: Fawcett Books, 1970.

Watzlawick, P., J.H. Weakland, and R. Fisch. *Change: Principles of Problem Formation and Problem Resolution.* New York: W.W. Norton, 1974.

Weinberg, G.M. *The Psychology of Computer Programming.* New York: Van Nostrand Reinhold, 1971.

Yourdon, E. *Managing the Structured Techniques,* 2nd ed. New York: Yourdon Press, 1979.

Index

Notes

Notes

Notes

Notes

Notes

Notes

.nnouncing. . . .

he Annual Prentice Hall Professional/Technical/Reference atalog: Books For Computer Scientists, omputer/Electrical Engineers and Electronic Technicians

rentice Hall, the leading publisher of Professional/Technical/Reference books in the world, s pleased to make its vast selection of titles in computer science, computer/electrical engineering and electronic technology more accessible to all professionals in these fields hrough the publication of this new catalog!

f your business or research depends on timely, state-of-the-art information, The Annual rentice Hall Professional/Technical/Reference Catalog: Books For Computer Scientists, Computer/Electrical Engineers and Electronic Technicians was designed especially for you! Titles appearing in this catalog will be grouped according to interest areas. Each entry will nclude: title, author, author affiliations, title description, table of contents, title code, page count and copyright year.

n addition, this catalog will also include advertisements of new products and services from other companies in key high tech areas.

SPECIAL OFFER!

- Order your copy of The Annual Prentice Hall Professional/Technical/Reference Catalog: Books For Computer Scientists, Computer/Electrical Engineers and Electronic Technicians for only $2.00 and receive $5.00 off the purchase of your first book from this catalog. In addition, this catalog entitles you to special discounts on Prentice Hall titles in computer science, computer/electrical engineering and electronic technology.

----

ase send me _____ copies of The Annual Prentice Hall Professional/Technical/Reference alog (title code: 62280–3)

VE!

ayment accompanies order, plus your state's sales tax where applicable, Prentice Hall pays postage and dling charges. Same return privilege refund guaranteed. Please do not mail cash.

☐ PAYMENT ENCLOSED—shipping and handling to be paid by publisher (please include your state's tax where applicable).
☐ BILL ME for The Annual Prentice Hall Professional/Technical/Reference Catalog (with small charge for shipping and handling).

l your order to: Prentice Hall, Book Distribution Center,
Route 59 at Brook Hill Drive,
West Nyack, N.Y. 10994

ne _____

ress _____

' _____ State _____ Zip _____

efer to charge my ☐ Visa ☐ MasterCard

d Number _____ Expiration Date _____

nature _____

Offer not valid outside the United States.

pt. 1

D-PPTR-CS(9)